STATES
Upper (ALTA) California
UPPER CALIFORNIA
Drake's Bay
SAN FRANCISCO de ASIS
SANTA CLARA
Bay of Monterey
CARMEL
SAN ANTONIO de PADUA
SAN LUIS OBISPO
Pacific Ocean
SAN BUENAVENTURA
SAN GABRIEL
SAN JUAN CAPISTRANO
SAN DIEGO
San Diego Bay
MEXICO
EXICO
Gulf of Mexico
JALPAN
GUADALAJARA
QUERETARO
MEXICO CITY
VERA CRUZ

SANDALS ON THE GOLDEN HIGHWAY

Padre Serra made the mission of San Carlos his headquarters.

SANDALS ON THE GOLDEN HIGHWAY

A Life of Junipero Serra

By

TERI MARTINI

Illustrations by Nino Carbe

ST. ANTHONY GUILD PRESS, PATERSON, NEW JERSEY

Library of Congress Catalog Card Number: 59-13344

Nihil obstat:

BEDE BABO, O. S. B.

Censor librorum.

Imprimatur:

✝ JAMES A. MCNULTY

Bishop of Paterson.

May 12, 1959

1959

PRINTED IN THE UNITED STATES OF AMERICA

For Carol

whose help and inspiration

have been invaluable

The characters depicted in this book are, with very few minor exceptions, persons who actually lived in Junipero Serra's time. The incidents narrated are based on authentic accounts of the life of Padre Serra: *Palou's Life of Junipero Serra,* translated and annotated by Maynard J. Geiger, O. F. M., and the *Writings of Junipero Serra,* Volumes I, II, and III, edited by Antonine Tibesar, O. F. M., all published by the Academy of American Franciscan History, Washington, D. C.; and *Historical Memoirs of New California by Fray Francisco Palou,* edited by Herbert E. Bolton, and published by the University of California Press, Berkeley, Calif.

For the sake of simplifying the reading of the text, no accents have been used on Spanish words.

Preface

THE story you are about to read, boys and girls, is that of a pioneer. His journeys, like those of all pioneers were difficult ones. He faced hunger, illness and hostile Indians with great courage. There was one important difference. Padre Junipero Serra was God's pioneer.

Padre Serra did not carry a gun. He did not ride in a covered wagon. He traveled on foot as a true Franciscan, his sandal-clad feet carrying him from place to place. It is thought that during his life in the New World he traveled more than twelve thousand miles, much of the time on foot. All he had to protect himself was his unfailing faith in God.

While England and France fought over claims to the New World in the East, the Spanish were busy in the West. They were establishing settlements in Mexico and along the California coast.

In the 1770's rebellious cries of "Taxation without representation," and "Give me liberty or give me death," echoed throughout the English colonies. And in 1776, with the Declaration of Independence, the United States was born.

At the same time a valiant little Friar was struggling to build the missions that would be the first permanent settlements in what is today the state of California.

Padre Serra's story is the story of the early years of the Golden State. Lame and no longer young, the little Friar began his long walk along the Royal Highway up the western coast of our country. He made it a Golden Highway dedicated to the King of kings. He strengthened it with a chain of nine missions. They stand today, their yellow adobe walls like a golden chain of love.

There are many colorful heroes in the history of the West. None was more courageous or determined than Junipero Serra, God's Pioneer.

* * *

There are many steps to be taken before an outstanding, holy man or woman can be declared a saint. The long process by which the Church examines the virtues of these holy people is called the cause of beatification and canonization. Padre Junipero Serra's cause was opened in December, 1948, in Fresno, California. It is now being studied at Rome.

—TERI MARTINI

Contents

Illustrations

PAGE

PRONUNCIATION GUIDE

Because many of the Spanish words and names in the book will be unfamiliar, this guide has been included. In the bold-face type the words have been spelled as they should be pronounced. The Castilian pronunciation of Spanish, which the missionaries taught the Indians, has been used here.

Alta — **ahl′ ta**

Amad a Dios, mis hijos — **Ah-math′ ah Dee-os′, mees ee′ hos**

Baja — **Bah′ ha**

Bucareli, Antonio — **Boo-ka-reh′ lee, An-toh′ nee-oh**

Cadiz — **Kah′ deeth**

Choquet, Diego — **Tcho-ket′, Dee-ay′ go**

Crespi, Padre Juan — **Kres′ pee, Pah′ dray Hwahn**

de Croix, Marques — **de Crwah, Mar-Kee′**

El Camino Real — **El Kah-mee′ no Reh-ahl′**

El Cojo — **El Ko′ ho**

Fages, Pedro — **Fah′ hes, Peh′ dro**

Figuer, Padre — **Fee-gair′, Pah′ dray**

Fray — **Fry**

Fuster, Padre — **Foos-tair′, Pah′ dray**

Galvez, Jose de — **Gahl′ veth, Ho-zay′ deh**

Gaviota — **Gah-vee-o′ tah**

Gomez, Padre — **Go′ meth, Pah′ dray**

Guadalajara — **Gwah-da-la-ha′ rah**

Jalpan — **Hal-pahn′**

Jayme, Padre Luis — **Ha′ ee-may, Pah′ dray Loo-ees′**

Jose — **Ho-zay′**

Juan — **Hwahn**

La Paz — **La Pahth**

Lasuen, Padre — **Lah-swen′, Pah′ dray**

Majorca — **Mah-yor′ ka**

Malaga — **Mah′ lah-gah**

Margarita — **Mar-gah-ree′ tah**

Miguel — **Mee-ghell′**

Monterey — **Mon-teh-ray′**

Neve, Felipe de — **Nay′ vay, Feh-lee′ pay deh**

Ortega, Jose Francisco — **Or-tay′ gah, Ho-zay′ Fran-thees′ ko**

Palou, Padre — **Pah-loo′, Pah′ dray**

Parron, Padre — **Par-ron′, Pah′ dray**

Paterno, Padre — **Pah-ter′ no, Pah′ dray**

Petra — **Peh′ trah**

Portola, Gaspar de — **Por-toh′ lah, Gahs-par′ deh**

Presidio — **preh-zee′ dee-o**

Queretaro — **Keh-reh′ tah-ro**

Rivera y Moncada, Fernando de — **Ree-veh′ rah ee Mon-cah′ dah, Fer-nahn′ do deh**

San Antonio — **Sahn Ahn-toh′ nee-o**

San Blas — **Sahn Blahs**

San Buenaventura — **Sahn Bway-nah-ben-too′ rah**

San Carlos — **Sahn Kar′ los**

Santa Clara — **Sahn′ tah Klah′ rah**

San Diego — **Sahn Dee-ay′ go**

San Francisco — **Sahn Frahn-thees′ ko**

San Gabriel — **Sahn Gah-bree-el′**

San Juan Capistrano — **Sahn Hwahn Kah-pees-trah′ no**

San Luis Obispo — **Sahn Loo-ees′ O-bees′ po**

Serra, Padre Junipero — **Ser′ rah, Pah′ dray Hoo-nee′ peh-ro**

Sierra Gorda — **See-er′ rah Gor′ dah**

Vaya con Dios — **Vah′ yah cone Dee-os′**

Velicata — **Veh-lee-kah′ tah**

Veracruz — **Veh′-rah krooth**

Vizcaino — **Veeth-kah-ee′ no**

Yuma — **Yoo′ ma**

Chapter One

"I am sixteen," he answered.

I . . . . . . Miguel Learns a Lesson

FATHER Provincial shifted the papers on his desk impatiently. He looked disapprovingly at the small, delicate boy standing before him.

"Miguel Serra," he said sternly, "entrance into the Order of St. Francis is a serious matter."

The boy nodded agreement quickly. His dark eyes flashed with excitement and real desire. This was a very important day. If Father Provincial approved, Miguel Jose Serra would become a Franciscan.

"Yes, Father Provincial," was all that Miguel could manage.

He wanted to tell the Provincial how long he had studied and how, more than anything else in the world, he wanted to serve God. If only his throat were not so dry he could tell how his mother and father had sacrificed to send him to study at Palma. They were proud to give their son to God.

But the Provincial seemed angry and annoyed. What could be wrong?

"Miguel Serra," he inquired, leaning across his desk and looking directly into the boy's steady brown eyes, "exactly how old are you?"

Miguel was not surprised. He knew that he was unusually small for his age. He had many scars to show that his size had caused him much discomfort. Boys his age could not help teasing one another. Sometimes they even went further, so that Miguel had to defend himself. More than once he had proved that his small stature was not a measure of his courage.

He drew himself up proudly now. "I am sixteen," he answered.

The Provincial's face flushed with exasperation. "Unbelievable!" he thought. "What sort of nonsense is this?"

It seemed impossible. Miguel Serra had certainly not reached the height of five feet. Besides, the boy looked frail. He must be in poor health. Surely anyone could see that he was not strong enough to enter a religious Order.

Miguel stood with downcast eyes. He was close to tears. The Provincial did not believe him. He would not be allowed to enter the Franciscan Order.

"All because I am too small," he thought bitterly.

Surely his size would not matter to God. Certainly God could see how full of love his heart was and how much he longed to serve the Divine Master. The boy trembled now as he heard the stern tone in the Provincial's voice.

"Life in the novitiate is hard, much too difficult for one so young and frail as yourself. I cannot approve your application."

Miguel turned without a word and left the small office. He could not let Father Provincial see the tears that stung his eyes. He was disgraced.

He walked through the streets of Palma blindly. At last he found himself at the waterfront. There the small sailing boats rocked to and fro in the gentle breeze. A clear blue sky smiled down upon the island of Majorca. The Mediterranean stretched and rippled into the distance as far as the eye could see. Surely this island off the coast of Spain was one of the most beautiful places in all the world.

Miguel could not appreciate that now. His eyes were dimmed by tears. He let them roll down his cheeks unnoticed. There was only one place he wanted to be.

On the waterfront, rising almost from the sea, stood the majestic Cathedral of Palma. Miguel hurried inside and threw himself upon his knees before the main altar.

The boy's thoughts turned to his family. As he knelt there the walls of the Cathedral seemed to melt away and he saw himself inside the poor, white stone house in Petra. Most of the people of Petra were farmers. Like them, the Serras owned farmlands outside the village. But the farmers of Petra liked having close neighbors, and so it was that their houses were side by side along the narrow streets of the village.

Now Miguel was thinking of a time several years earlier: ... he had been lying upon his bed in the little alcove near his parents' bedroom. He had opened his eyes to find the family at his side.

"Dear Lord, don't let my brother die," his sister, Juana, was sobbing.

"My son, my son," cried a man's voice. That was his father, Antonio Serra.

"Hush," said Margarita. She put her cool hand on her son's burning forehead and smiled reassuringly.

"The fever will go. I know this in my heart. God has chosen my son for His work. Sleep now, Miguel. Tomorrow all will be well."

Miguel had closed his eyes gratefully. And the next morning the fever was gone. Within a few days he was performing his small duties on his father's farm outside the village once again.

But there had not been much time for working the land. For Miguel was studying with the Friars of San Bernardino in Petra. And as he studied and prayed he found a growing desire in his heart to become a Franciscan himself. He had progressed rapidly at school, and soon it had been arranged for him to go to Palma to begin his higher education. Now, after a short time in the city, he had decided to wait no longer before applying to the Provincial for admission into the Franciscan Order. But it seemed as if the Order did not want him. The Provincial, who was in charge of all the Franciscans on Majorca, had turned him down.

* * *

Miguel knelt in the Cathedral, thinking it all over. He wondered what would happen next. Had he worked so hard for nothing? Had his family prayed and sacrificed in vain?

Suddenly Miguel felt a hand upon his shoulder. He looked up into the kindly face of an elderly priest. The priest had noticed Miguel when the boy had entered the church nearly two hours before. He motioned Miguel to follow him and led the boy outside to the stone steps.

As they left the Cathedral Miguel was surprised to notice that it was evening already. How long he must have been inside!

"I could not help noticing someone in such distress," the kindly priest told Miguel. "Would you like to talk over your problem with me? Perhaps I can help."

Miguel was grateful for the kind offer, and after a moment's hesitation he poured out the whole story. The old priest could not help being impressed by the boy's sincerity. He tried his best to cheer Miguel and encourage him.

"It seems to me that there is some misunderstanding here. I'm sure your friends at the monastery will speak to the Provincial about you. Why, in a very short time, the Provincial may even wish to see you again and reconsider his decision," he told the boy.

This was certainly logical and it did make Miguel feel a little better. Still, he could not be as confident as his new friend. But he needn't have worried. For, within a few days, the Provincial did ask to see him.

This time Father Provincial looked at Miguel even more closely than before. He shook his head at last and sighed.

"Miguel Serra, you are unbelievably small for one who has reached the age of sixteen."

"Oh, Your Reverence, I will grow. There is still time. I'm sure of it," insisted the boy.

The Provincial smiled at Miguel's eagerness.

"A man is small only if he is small inside," he said. "The Friars who know you best tell me that your devotion is strong. That is the finest of recommendations. It is far more important to grow spiritually than physically."

"And now, in view of the fact that your intention is good and you have a fine record in your studies, you will be allowed to enter the Order of St. Francis on September 14 at the Friary of Jesus."

And so it was on that day in 1730 that Miguel Jose Serra was clothed in the habit of the Franciscan Order. The habit was a rough robe of a grayish-brown color called *marrone.* It was fastened at the waist with a rope. On his feet the young Friar wore sandals. His head had been shaved at the top so that only a circle of hair was left.

Miguel was the smallest postulant there that day, but for once he did not mind. He felt as though he were glowing inside.

A year later, on September 15, 1731, Miguel made his religious profession in the Franciscan Order. It was a proud day for Margarita and Antonio Serra. Their son looked magnificent to them in his Franciscan robes. He had a new name now — Fray (meaning Brother or Friar) Junipero. Junipero had been the name of St. Francis' humble and amusing companion. The new Fray Junipero wanted to be as much like his namesake as possible.

A new name, a new life and a heart brimming over with love and thanksgiving. These were the things that counted most. Fray Junipero knew this because on that day he felt bigger than anyone, inside.

Chapter Two

"I am the one from our province who intends to make this journey," Padre Serra told his friend.

II . . . . . . Padre Junipero's Secret

JUNIPERO Serra had a secret which he kept hidden in his heart. It was something of which he dared not speak, not yet anyway. But there were times when his eyes had grown so weary of study that he rested them for a short while. Then it was that his secret hope and dream crept into his thoughts and he yearned for the day when it could come true.

It seemed a long time ago that the idea first presented itself. For as long as he could remember it had been with him. He often thought back several years to the days when little Miguel Jose Serra had first come to Palma. Fray Junipero had to smile when he thought of the word "little." No one had believed he would grow any more.

As a novice he had been too small and frail for hard work. His superiors had assigned him simple tasks about the altar, such as serving Mass for the Friar priests. But Fray Junipero did grow. Although he would never be thought of as tall, at least no one took him for a child any more.

At first the other boys had thought him too small to participate in their sports. Some had even made fun of him. But Fray Junipero had a wonderful sense of humor and the ability to laugh at his own mistakes. He made friends in his own way.

He was fun to be with, and in addition, he was a wonderful storyteller. His new friends never tired of hearing tales of the sea and far-off places that he had learned from the sailors who docked in the ports of Majorca.

After his profession in the Order, Fray Junipero was sent to another friary in Palma to study philosophy and theology in preparation for becoming a priest.

Sometimes he and his friends went to hear lectures by visiting missionaries. It would have been difficult to be unmoved by these sincere Friars who came to speak to them.

"Teachers and scholars are necessary to Holy Mother Church," the missionaries said, "but just as important is the winning of new souls for God. All over the world there are thousands of souls waiting to be brought to God."

Fray Junipero was well acquainted with the lives of missionaries and martyrs. He read them over and over again. He retained them in memory nearly word for word. He admired these men because they had given all they had to God, their very lives. More than anything else he wanted to imitate their perfect devotion to our Saviour.

At last, in 1737, Fray Junipero was ordained to the priesthood. Now he had the special power, given by Our Lord Himself, to offer the Holy Sacrifice of the Mass. His hands were consecrated with holy oil. Whatever these hands would bless, would be blessed by God. From this time on Junipero was called Padre (or Father).

Even after ordination Padre Junipero continued to keep secret his desire to be a missionary. He must learn to be a good Franciscan before he could do anything more.

Into this task he put his whole heart. He had an unusually brilliant mind. When he was still a young priest, he was assigned to teach philosophy at the friary of San Francisco in Palma, where he himself had studied before ordination. It was while he was teaching this course that he made two lifelong friends, Francisco Palou and Juan Crespi.

These two young students for the priesthood looked up to Father Serra and admired him very much. They spent many hours in his company, but not even to them did Padre Serra confide his secret.

As time went on, Junipero Serra continued to gain honors. He obtained a doctor's degree from the Lullian University in Palma. So excellent was his record at the University that in 1744 he was given the important professorship of Scotist Philosophy there. Among the older professors there was talk that Padre Junipero Serra would go far in the Church.

"A mind such as his is rare," they said.

"Imagine, a farm boy from Petra! Perhaps he will one day head the Order."

"Who knows, he may be the future Bishop of Majorca!" they suggested.

But Padre Junipero was not looking for important positions. He only did, as well as he could, the work that God gave him. As the years went on and he worked hard at being a good teacher, the desire to work among the pagans began to fade from his mind. Then, twelve years after Padre Junipero's ordination something happened to bring his thoughts back to missionary work.

In 1749 the Franciscan Order sent out a new call for volunteers to become missionaries in the New World. When Padre Serra heard of this, his old longing returned, this time stronger than ever. He spoke of his wish to his Superiors but he told none of his close friends. He prayed that God would choose him, and he began a novena, begging that if it were God's will He might stir the heart of someone at the monastery to join him as a companion.

One day as Padre Serra made his way across the quadrangle after class, things began to happen. He walked slowly, admiring the beautiful Majorcan day. The trees and building stood out sharply in the clear, sparkling sunshine. He thought of his friend, Francisco Palou, now an ordained priest. He wished Francisco could share an hour of this lovely day with him. He hurried to the friary and knocked at the door of the young priest's cell.

Francisco was delighted to see his friend.

"I am so glad you have come. I have been wanting to speak to you for some time about a matter of the greatest importance to me." Here Padre Palou hesitated. He seemed both worried and excited.

"Come, come, Francisco," encouraged Padre Serra. "We have always been able to speak freely with one another. Perhaps I can find some way to help you. Now, tell me what is troubling you."

The young Friar smiled with gratitude.

"Not long ago, when a call for more missionaries to New Spain went out," he confided, "I heard that someone from this very province was planning to go. No one seemed to know exactly who it was, but the more I thought about it, the more I felt that I, too, would like to engage in this work."

Padre Serra was so surprised he could not speak.

Father Palou became very serious now. "I know I have never spoken to you about this, but for some time I have longed to work in the foreign missions. And now the opportunity has presented itself. I only regret that we would have to be separated. I want to ask your advice before requesting permission from our Superiors to go.

"It seems — " Padre Palou continued, but here he had to stop, for something had come over Padre Serra. There was a very strange look on his face and tears had filled his eyes.

Padre Palou was horrified. He hardly knew what to do. Leading Padre Serra to a bench, he made him sit down, speaking nervously all the while. "Forgive me, dear friend. How could I be so inconsiderate! Sit here, please. What can I do?"

But it was some moments before Padre Serra found his voice. "I am the one from our province who intends to make this journey," he cried at last.

Tears of joy blinded him. All those long years of waiting and praying seemed very worth while. Not only was he to become a missionary in the New World, but his cherished friend had also received God's call and would be his companion. It was almost too much happiness at once.

Padre Serra and Padre Palou were among the first from Majorca to volunteer.

The news traveled rapidly through the University and among all the Friars in Palma. Soon everyone knew what Padre Palou and Padre Serra had done. Very few approved of their action. It was especially hard for the professors at the University to give up the great plans they had made for Padre Junipero Serra.

"It is sheer foolishness to waste such brilliant minds on ignorant natives," they said. "We need scholars here; they ought not to be buried somewhere in the wilderness."

Many tried to reason with the determined pair, but it was useless.

Although the two Friars had written at once to the Commissary General, who was in charge of Franciscan missions in the New World, the time for departure grew closer and closer and no word of their appointment came. Padre Palou became very worried.

"Can it be that we will not be included in the expedition?" he asked Padre Serra apprehensively.

And then the answer came. It was long and formal, but the meaning of the reply was simple enough.

"... We regret that the Commissary already has a sufficient number of volunteers, but we will keep your applications in mind in case of a vacancy."

The professors and students and many of the Friars were secretly pleased. Now their treasured Padre Serra would stay with them.

Only Padre Juan Crespi was sorry. When he had heard of his friends' decision to apply for missionary work, he began to think. Soon he was certain that he, too, would like to join them. Perhaps the Commissary would take him with another group as soon as possible. But now it seemed as if none of them would be going.

Padre Palou was crushed and deeply discouraged. He felt bitter disappointment. "Perhaps it was never meant to be. Perhaps we should forget all about it," he said to Padre Serra.

The little Friar only smiled gently. "You forget, Francisco — it is God who has called us to this work. We must await His answer."

To Padre Palou it seemed that God had already given His answer. On the other hand, Padre Serra was not the least bit discouraged. He was sent to his own village of Petra to preach during the Lenten season. He was very happy with the assignment, for he felt that perhaps this would be his last opportunity to see his family.

It was springtime in Petra. There was little change in the climate in Majorca because the weather there is always warm and pleasant. Nevertheless, there was the feeling of new life. The grass was greener and the orchard trees had begun to blossom. High overhead, flocks of yellow canaries flew through the clear air.

Padre Junipero was glad to be home again. Everyone was delighted to see this celebrated relative and old friend.

"Mamma, Papa, how well you look!" he exclaimed.

"You look so strong, Miguel. Surely the university life agrees with you," said Margarita, proudly surveying her son.

Padre Serra began to tell them how often he thought with longing of the pleasant days he had spent in Petra. Then three handsome children entered the room, laughing and excited. When they saw their uncle in his long gray robes they hung back, suddenly shy. But shyness vanished almost immediately as their mother ran forward and embraced her brother.

"Well! You haven't changed a bit since I was home last," Padre Serra told his sister, Juana. "But who are these three young strangers? Surely they are not members of the Serra family. I don't believe they know me."

With that the children began to laugh and, running to their beloved uncle, grasped his hands and hugged him fondly.

Padre Serra had hardly a moment to himself. There was a daily parade of relatives and friends coming to see him. At last he was able to take several quiet walks with his father and brother-in-law about the farmlands and discuss the planting of new crops.

Everything he saw and everyone he spoke to seemed more precious to Padre Serra, for he had a strong feeling that this would be the last time he could be with his family and friends. Still he spoke to no one of his secret hope of obtaining missionary work in the New World. He kept it all to himself, for he loved these people too much to be able to say good-by to them.

In Palma, Padre Palou had almost given up all hope of being called to the New World. But at Cadiz unforeseen events were taking place. Here the thirty-three volunteers selected for the expedition to Mexico were awaiting the arrival of their ship. Five of these Franciscans were men who had never before seen the sea. Terrified at the sight of the waves tossing the small ships about, they asked to be excused. They feared that they would never be able to make the long journey and therefore would be of no use to the Order.

To the Commissary General of the Indies this was a very great disappointment. It was necessary for him to look through his applications for men to replace these Friars. Among the applications he found the names of Padre Junipero Serra and Padre Francisco Palou. He sent for the two Friars immediately.

March 30, 1749, was Palm Sunday. Padre Palou was just going to the Blessing of the Palms when news of the appointments reached him. He set out that very day for Petra to tell his friend that the dream they shared had come true. He was only sorry that he had not had more faith that his prayers would be answered.

When Padre Serra greeted his friend in Petra, he knew that something important had happened, but he hardly dared put his hopes into words.

"Francisco, how wonderful! I'm glad you came. Everyone will be so happy to see you," he cried. Then he hesitated. "But surely —— Could there be a particular reason for your visit?" he asked hopefully.

Padre Palou smiled slyly. He knew very well what his friend was thinking and he couldn't resist teasing him a little. "Just some news," he replied carelessly. "It can wait, of course." But the twinkle and excitement in his eyes had given him away.

Tears filled Padre Serra's eyes. "God be praised," he cried joyfully. "He has called us at last."

Together the two friends began making plans. And so Miguel Jose Serra took leave of his family for the very last time without telling them of his appointment. He knew it would cause his aging parents too much suffering to make last farewells.

It was hard to leave old friends at Palma. Padre Juan Crespi was especially sad. He wished he were going too. Padre Serra tried to cheer him up.

"Perhaps it will not be too long before you join us, Juan. I shall pray for you. Nothing would add more to my happiness than to have you with us," he said.

On April 13, 1749, Padre Serra left Palma after twenty years there and set out for Malaga on a packet boat with Padre Palou. Padre Serra was already over thirty-five years old, yet in one sense his life was only beginning.

The dream he had held in his heart years before, and had then almost forgotten, was to come true at last. Soon everyone in Majorca would know of his desire for missionary work. And in years to come, though this was furthest from his thoughts, the name of Junipero Serra would be familiar the world over.

What lay ahead in the New World? Were the tales about hostile Indians true? Could these souls be won for God? The two Franciscans did not know. They were only proud and happy that God had chosen them for this work.

Chapter Three

In the heat of his anger the Captain suddenly produced a long, glittering dagger and threatened the small Friar with it.

III . . . . Trouble on Board

APRIL 13 was a fine day. The ships rocked gently to and fro in the wind at the port of Palma.

"A perfect day to begin our new adventure," remarked Padre Palou.

"It is indeed," replied Padre Serra as they prepared to embark upon the English packet boat that would carry them to Malaga. From there they would travel to the Spanish port of Cadiz, where the other missionaries awaited them. Just then they became aware of frantic cries behind them.

"Padres, Padres, wait, please wait."

The two Friars turned to see a Majorcan sailor rushing towards them. He reached them breathing heavily from running. His face was flushed and he found it difficult to talk. Padre Serra looked up at the strong young man.

"What is it, my son?"

"Padre, I beg of you, do not take that ship. In a day or two there will be another ship to take you to Malaga."

"What can be the trouble? The ship is seaworthy, is it not? It is very important that we reach Cadiz as soon as possible," said Padre Palou, somewhat perplexed.

"Oh, certainly it is seaworthy," replied the sailor. "But, believe me, Padres, it would be better for you to wait. The captain of this ship is a very strange man. I fear for your safety. But, please — what difference will a day or two make? If you like, I will find you suitable passage myself."

Padre Serra smiled kindly. "We appreciate your concern, my son. We have already heard about this captain. We are not worried. Padre Palou and I have important work in the New World. We intend to get there safely. There is no time to waste."

The young sailor shook his head sadly. "You are very brave. But I don't think that you realize the danger. I pray God for your safety."

"Thank you," said Padre Serra gratefully. "God will bless you and we shall be quite safe."

Nevertheless he and Padre Palou boarded the packet boat with some misgivings. Nearly everyone with whom they had spoken had warned them against this captain. The man was nowhere to be seen that day. The mate showed them to their tiny, cramped quarters.

"There are times," sighed Father Serra, "when I am almost glad of my small stature."

"Yes, that certainly will be an advantage here," laughed Padre Palou rather nervously. Then he added in an undertone: "About this captain. What do you really think? Perhaps he is a madman."

"I think, Francisco, that we can only wait and see. Hope for the best," added Padre Serra.

That night neither of them slept very well. The very next morning the Friars encountered the Captain on deck. He was indeed an unusual-looking man. His ruddy complexion and wild, wind-blown hair made him a perfect picture of a madman. His strange way of speaking did not improve this first impression either. The Captain spoke only English well and knew Portuguese very slightly. It was very difficult to understand him. His manners were certainly terrible.

"Fools!" he shouted, "what do you think you are doing dressed like that?" regarding their Franciscan robes with disdain. "If I had my way all you Friars would be at the bottom of the sea." He waved his arms about so threateningly that Padre Serra and Padre Palou were rooted to the spot.

Suddenly the Captain drew a Bible from his blouse. He began quoting Scripture and shouting arguments at them. "What does that mean, and that?" he screamed.

Without waiting for an answer he would go on to another passage. The ship's crew and the other passengers had become strangely quiet. The Captain was working himself into a frenzy. What could the Friars do against this man who was evidently filled with a violent hatred?

He stepped forward menacingly. Padre Palou grasped his friend's arm and tried to pull him back. Why hadn't they listened to the sailor's warning?

"So you are traveling to Malaga, eh? What makes you think you will ever reach that port?" roared the Captain.

To everyone's surprise Padre Serra stepped forward and approached the raving man. He spoke in a soothing voice as if to a little child. "We have no wish to argue with you, Captain. We are very sorry our presence here disturbs you, but we can keep out of your way as much as possible. As for reaching Malaga — " here Padre Serra paused.

At this Padre Palou, taking courage, stepped forward. "As for reaching Malaga," he said firmly, "we are expected there. I believe there would be some very embarrassing questions for you to answer if we were not among the passengers when this ship arrives. Our king would make demands of the King of England and you would pay with your head."

At these words the Captain suddenly turned on his heel and strode off. There was relief in Padre Palou's eyes as he turned to his friend. "For a moment there, I was certain we would not live to see the New World. I was nearly paralyzed with fear."

Padre Serra brought out two trembling hands from beneath his robe. "You were not the only one, Francisco."

During the two weeks of the voyage the Friars spent most of their time in their quarters. But each time he did meet Padre Serra the Captain would produce his Bible. He seemed to delight in arguing. Choosing a passage at random, he would begin to interpret the meaning according to his own ideas. Quietly, but firmly, Padre Serra would cite other passages in order to point out the Captain's mistakes. This only made the man more angry than ever. He would search the Bible frantically for yet another quotation to prove the point as he saw it. Finding none, he would shout that there was such a text but the page was missing from his copy of the Scriptures.

One night while Padre Palou was sleeping, the Captain sought out Padre Serra alone. In the heat of his anger, he suddenly produced a long, glittering dagger and threatened the small Friar with it. Padre Serra showed no fear. He stood his ground. Something stayed the Captain's hand and he left suddenly in a terrible fury.

Padre Serra went to his friend and woke him at once. He recounted what had happened and the two priests lay awake all night expecting the Captain to return and kill them both. But he did not return. And for the rest of the voyage he did not annoy them as much as before.

At last the harrowing trip was over. Padre Serra and his companion stopped at a friary in Malaga for five days before they could get a small sailing boat to Cadiz.

At Cadiz a time of restless waiting began. Eighteen other Friars waited with them. An ocean voyage was a very dangerous undertaking in those days. Many of these Friars knew little of the sea except the wild stories they had been hearing ever since their journey had been planned. Padre Serra was considered an expert on the subject, having come from an island village. He did what he could to reassure these young missionaries.

"I have heard that there are terrible storms at sea where the waves become like mountains and capsize the ship," one young man confided to Padre Serra.

"And what about the calms?" questioned another. "I have heard that ships sometimes stay in one place for weeks without a breath of wind. Then food runs out and the sailors are never heard of again."

At times like these Padre Serra would recall all the ships that had made numerous safe voyages in spite of these hazards. Everyone listened eagerly, hoping that this trip would be as successful. But the longer they had to wait, the more worried they became.

Padre Serra took advantage of this time to write to his family in Petra. He addressed his letter to his cousin, who would read it to the others. Now he told them all of his plans and promised to remember them daily at Mass.

Finally, at the end of August, 1749, they were under way. Fears were for the time forgotten in the excitement of setting out on their mission. It was a splendid day. A stiff breeze filled the sails and everyone was eager for adventure.

Padre Junipero Serra breathed deeply of the fresh sea air. His chest swelled and his shoulders were drawn back. He stood poised and ready, stretching himself to the full measure of his five feet two inches. And still he felt very small indeed when faced with the enormous expanse of the Atlantic Ocean.

There was a soft chuckle and Padre Palou came up beside him. "Are you planning to join the gulls?" he asked, nodding towards the birds circling above. Indeed, to look at him, anyone would have thought the little Friar was preparing for flight.

Padre Serra's eyes twinkled. "Joining the gulls would only bring me back to Cadiz," he answered. "No, I would rather be borne upon the back of a sea monster if it would bring me to the New World sooner, Francisco."

"It appears to me you already have that wish," remarked the younger man, looking about him with distaste.

The ship was not a new one and its scanty accommodations were filled to overflowing with Dominican and Franciscan missionaries bound for Mexico. It did not promise to be a very comfortable trip.

Padre Serra refused to let this dampen his spirits. It was a balmy August day, and the wind that whipped the gray robes about his legs was filling the sails and bringing him ever closer to a dream come true.

Padre Serra was a good sailor. He wasn't seasick and thus he was able to go about cheering up the other passengers. As time went on, it was very, very difficult to be cheerful. The food was terrible. Of course, there was no refrigeration in ships of those days, and so the meat they had was usually dried salt pork.

As if this was not bad enough, drinking water had to be rationed out each day. It was dirty and slimy but everyone was glad to get it. Many people got sick with scurvy. Padre Palou and Padre Serra went about nursing those who had fallen ill.

There were stormy days and days of calm and endless work to be done for the sick. Still Padre Serra never complained or spoke of fear. But Padre Palou noticed that his friend clasped a crucifix in his hands and slept with it on his breast each night.

Hard and dangerous as it was, the journey was not proving to be an unusually difficult one for those days. But one night after the ship had left Puerto Rico, a terrible storm arose. The wind howled and giant waves tossed the vessel about unmercifully. The Captain, realizing that he had been thrown hopelessly off course, gave up all hope of reaching Mexico.

The sad news reached the missionaries who were huddled in their quarters. There were tears in Padre Serra's eyes as he looked about him at the dejected passengers. "Have we come so close only to fail?" he whispered to Padre Palou. A hush came over the voyagers as they began to pray.

Suddenly one of the Friars spoke up. "Listen, everyone. I have an idea. Let us choose one *particular* saint and all pray to him or her."

"Good," the others answered, "but which saint?"

Everyone had a different idea. Padre Serra favored St. Francis Solanus because it was the example of this great missionary to Peru he was trying to follow in his own work. Meanwhile the storm outside raged and the little ship lurched violently.

"I know," said one missionary. "Let us each write a saint's name on paper and we will draw the name of our patron from a hat."

This plan was quickly agreed upon. The names were written down and one was drawn.

"Santa Barbara!" announced the missionary who held the scrap of paper aloft. The cry was taken up: "Hail, Santa Barbara!"

Strange to tell, at that very instant, as suddenly as the storm had come up, a calm settled. Two days later, singing hymns of praise and thanksgiving, the passengers watched their battered and badly leaking ship limp into the port of Veracruz. The voyage had lasted ninety days and they had disembarked not a moment too soon. The ship would not have lasted another day.

Ever afterward the day of the terrible storm was spoken of in awed voices. For it had been December 4 when the missionaries had put themselves under St. Barbara's protection and had been saved. December 4 was the very day the Church had set aside as St. Barbara's feast.

The Friars were made comfortable at a monastery in Veracruz. Many of them were too ill and weak to begin the land journey to Mexico City for some time. A Solemn High Mass of thanksgiving was sung and Padre Serra, as the most learned of the company, was chosen to deliver the sermon.

When it was time to begin the trip to Mexico City, a new problem presented itself. How were the Friars to travel?

In imitation of Christ's apostles, Franciscans went to and from their missions on foot as much as possible. This was directed in the Rule of St. Francis. Horseback riding was forbidden to the Friars except in cases of necessity or illness, and in Europe this rule could be generally observed. But here in the New World the distances between missions were tremendous. It was about two hundred and seventy miles from Veracruz to Mexico City. What was to be done? The problem was brought to Padre Serra.

But the little Friar could see no problem at all. "It is very simple," he said. "Those who are too ill will ride in wagons or on mules. As for myself, and my other strong friends," he added, looking around with a twinkle in his eye at Padre Palou and another young priest of whom he had become very fond, "we shall walk."

Walk! The Friars of Veracruz were shocked. "Walk, Padre?" they asked. "Walk two hundred and seventy miles over mountains and deserts in a strange land? It is impossible."

"Walk," repeated Padre Serra firmly, although his lips betrayed his amusement in a gentle smile. "St. Francis would not burden the poor animals with his body. We are Franciscans and we will follow his example."

Padre Palou and the other young Friar were eager to begin this journey. "Do not become too excited," Padre Serra teased his new friend. "Padre Palou and I don't want to have to lead a sleepwalker to Mexico City. Get a good night's rest." They were all in high spirits at the prospect.

But that night Padre Serra noticed that Padre Palou scarcely touched his food. Coming away from the table, he stumbled and nearly fell.

"Francisco, what is it? Are you ill?" asked Padre Serra, his voice filled with concern. Between them he and a young Friar led Padre Palou to his bed.

"Stop fussing," protested Padre Palou. "I'm perfectly all right, just excited." He laughed. "Perhaps I will be the sleepwalker you will have to lead."

No one laughed the next morning. During the night Padre Palou had developed a terrible fever. It was clear that he would not be going anywhere for quite some time. He was bitterly disappointed at having to be left behind. And he tried to hide this by making jokes.

"Well, you will be happy to learn that your sleepwalker will be doing his sleepwalking in bed," he told Padre Serra when the latter came in to say good-by. "But don't think you can get rid of me. I will be in Mexico City, perhaps even before you."

Padre Palou looked so pale and forlorn that his friend could hardly keep the sadness and worry from his voice. He thought back to the days of planning and hoping before their appointment had come. Francisco was to be his companion in the New World. Together they would have begun their first long journey in this new land. And now Francisco had to be left behind.

"Things don't always work out the way we plan. But what has happened is God's will. We shall meet in Mexico City."

Sadly the two friends parted. Padre Serra began his long walk. Mexico City was a great distance away. But he would have even farther to walk before his work was finished.

Chapter Four

"Walk along the bank until I show you where to cross," said the man.

IV . . The Long Road to Mexico City

HIGH on the Central Plateau, more than seven thousand feet above sea level, stands the ancient Aztec stronghold of Mexico City. After Cortes took over the city in 1521, the beautiful Indian buildings and temples were destroyed. In their place the Spaniards built magnificent churches, palaces and plazas.

When Padre Junipero Serra set out on foot to reach the city in 1749, it was a very wealthy and perhaps wicked city. The Spanish nobles and ladies were chiefly interested in their own comfort. Most of their work was carried on by Indian and Negro slaves.

Just outside the city was the large Apostolic College of San Fernando. Here it was that many missionaries from Europe were trained for their work in the New World. At San Fernando Padre Palou anxiously awaited the arrival of his friends just as he had said he would. Weakened from his illness, he had been forced to ride with some of the others, thus completing the journey more quickly than the two Franciscans who traveled on foot.

The Rector of the University was amazed by the news Padre Palou had brought him. "But you must be joking," he told the young missionary. "I cannot believe that anyone would be so foolhardy as to attempt the long journey from Veracruz on foot. Not only on foot but without provisions of any kind. I fear we may never see these Friars."

"On the contrary," Padre Palou corrected gently, "they have the best provisions of all, a staunch faith in God to provide them with whatever is necessary. They will come."

Even as Padre Palou was speaking the travelers were plodding successfully toward their destination.

The journey had started off easily enough. At first the travelers were able to keep to the road on the plain just outside Veracruz. The countryside was beautiful. Wild flowers and fruit grew in abundance.

"I don't think I have ever tasted anything so delicious," exclaimed Padre Serra's companion, savoring some juicy berries.

Padre Junipero laughed. "That is what comes of living on a diet of dried salt pork for so many months."

"Perhaps, but doesn't it seem to you that they taste especially sweet? And what do you think? Shall we spend the night in the open? It doesn't seem likely that we shall find many people living hereabouts," commented the young Friar.

Padre Serra was delighted by his companion's enthusiasm. "The nights are cooler as we climb higher. You may be very happy to find shelter," he chuckled.

Padre Serra was right. Mexico's surface is varied. The countryside is continually changing from plain to highland to plateau. With it the climate changes from hot to cool and back again. Along the way the Friars were fortunate to find little villages and sometimes lonely huts. The natives were kind and friendly, giving food and shelter and directions for the next day's journey.

Once the two Friars were told they would have to cross a river before reaching a town where they could stay that night. It was already evening when they reached the river. But it was too wide to cross at this point.

"What can we do?" asked the young Padre. "There is not a sign of life in any direction." And he pulled his habit more tightly about him, for it was becoming very chilly.

Padre Serra shook his head, puzzled. "There must be a narrower place nearby. But in which direction, I cannot tell."

The idea of spending the night in the open was not as tempting as it had been at first. They had seen and heard wild animals along the way. Whether or not they were dangerous, the Friars did not know.

"Let us say a prayer to Our Lady for guidance," suggested Padre Serra.

Suddenly, out of nowhere, just as they finished, a figure could be vaguely seen moving on the other side of the river.

"Is that really a human being, or do I imagine it?" asked the young Friar.

Waiting no longer to find out, Padre Serra called out across the river for help. "I am ready to assist you," replied a man's voice in perfect Spanish. "What is it that you want?"

When he learned of their need, the man answered clearly: "There is nothing to fear. Walk along the bank until I show you where to cross."

Padre Serra indicated to his companion that they should start walking again. The two Friars kept a parallel course to the man on the other side of the river, guided only by his voice. Soon it was too dark to see anything at all of their strange, unknown guide.

The mysterious voice led them on. At last they reached a narrow place in the river where they would be able to cross easily.

The young Friar breathed a long sigh of relief. "How can we thank this man when we do not know who he is?"

At that moment a well-dressed Spaniard stepped into view. He greeted them politely and waved aside their thanks. "Follow me," he said and turned without another word.

The Friars looked at one another in wonder. The man made no further explanation. They decided to do as he said. He led them to a house quite a distance from the river. Here he offered them food and shelter for the night. He asked no questions and volunteered no information. Padre Serra and his companion were puzzled but grateful for the man's kindness.

The next morning they found that a cold rain had fallen during the night and covered the road with ice.

"What a great blessing we were given! Surely we would have perished if it had not been for this kind gentleman," exclaimed Padre Serra's companion.

Everywhere they went they found friends who were kind to them. It wasn't until their journey was almost over that something happened that was to affect Padre Serra for the rest of his life. They had suffered hunger and thirst. They had been lost and tired. They had survived disease and danger. It was from a seemingly harmless incident that Padre Serra became ill. While passing through a tropical area the missionaries were plagued by mosquitoes.

"Really, I have never seen such large insects," exclaimed the younger priest. "They keep me awake with their incessant buzzing all night. And how these bites itch!"

Padre Serra agreed wholeheartedly. The insect pests were annoying. For several days a particularly large bite on his leg had bothered him. He had noticed only this morning that during the night he must have frantically scratched his leg while he slept and it had been bleeding. It seemed to be swollen now and a little stiff. It was becoming harder and harder to keep up with his young friend's loping pace. But he said nothing.

By evening the infection had really taken hold. It was December and they had only a week's march before reaching the College of San Fernando. Padre Serra did not intend to stop now.

His companion could not help noticing the very pronounced limp. When they set out the next morning, Padre Serra was pale and unusually quiet. The young priest set a very slow pace. Then suddenly he stopped.

"Come, come, I am not so old that we must crawl to Mexico City," Padre Serra managed to smile.

"We are not going to walk or crawl another inch until something is done about you. You are ill, whether you will admit it or not." The young missionary held up his hand. "Not a word of argument, please. Now, turn right around because we are going back to the nearest village until you are well."

The young man spoke boldly because he was frightened. "In my eagerness to reach our destination I was too selfish to think of my companion. Now he is ill and it is my fault.

He would never complain. I should have been more observant," he thought.

His heart sank when he realized Padre Serra's weakness as the Friar leaned against him. They made their way slowly back to the village.

After a day of rest the fever left and the infection seemed to have cleared up. There was still a sore on his leg, but Padre Serra insisted upon continuing the journey.

"Very well," agreed his companion. "Our friends here have offered to give us a mule. You can ride and I will walk beside you."

Padre Serra would not hear of it. "I am surprised at you," he said. "Our father St. Francis meant for us to walk. That was our plan. I can't let a little mosquito bite stop me." He spoke gently, but his lips were firmly set.

His companion had learned to know that determined look. He realized there would be no point in arguing. And so it was that on New Year's Day, 1750, two dusty, weary travelers arrived at San Fernando. The younger man measured his gait to the painful limping of his friend.

A small group of Friars, along with Padre Palou and the Rector himself, rushed out to meet them.

"I can hardly believe it," exclaimed the Rector. "But here they are. Such determination! Such faith! We could all take a lesson from these valiant Friars."

When he was introduced to Padre Junipero Serra, one of the Friars cried out: "Oh, if only someone would bring us a forest of such 'junipers.' " Long before, St. Francis, speaking to his companion Brother Juniper, had made the same word play on "juniper" as a man's name and a tree.

San Fernando trained missionaries for work among the Indians. And Padre Junipero's example of following the Rule even under hardships was a fine one for the other Friars to follow. The Rector wished that all his missionaries could be like this Juniper.

"Francisco! How well you look! I am so glad to see you," cried Padre Serra.

For a while it seemed that everyone was talking at once in the excitement. The story of the long journey was told over and over again. It was a joyous occasion. But when Padre Palou heard about his friend's misfortune, he was very upset.

"We must send to the city at once for a doctor. The infection may appear to be cleared up, but that is a very decided limp. You can't hide it. The wound definitely needs attention," he told his friend.

"Now, Francisco," Padre Serra chided, "you and my companion have entered a conspiracy. This is nonsense. I am perfectly all right. The wound is not serious. It will be gone before you know it. Now let us hear no more about it. Agreed?"

Padre Serra sounded so sure that nothing was really wrong that Padre Palou began to feel foolish. "Very well," he said reluctantly.

"Fine! Now tell me what you have been doing and what our life here will be like. I am eager to hear everything."

The Friars would remain at the College for a time to prepare for their work with the Indians, Padre Serra knew. He realized that this was a prudent plan. In this way they would learn more about the Indian customs and something of the Indian dialects. At the same time they would prepare in other ways for the missionary work they had traveled so far to perform.

For five months Padre Serra and Padre Palou studied at the College of San Fernando. Then one day during the recreation hour they and several other Franciscans from Spain were gathered together in the garden. The Father Guardian in charge of the College was among them.

"I cannot tell you how happy I am to have you here. So many are needed and yet there are so few volunteers for this work." His eyes shone with joy.

"Perhaps some of you will wish to work among the Indians of the Sierra Gorda missions, where priests are especially needed right now." Padre Serra caught his friend's eye. Francisco smiled back. Without hesitation the small Friar spoke, quoting Scripture.

"Behold, here am I; send me."

Padre Palou immediately followed his friend's example, as did several others. Father Guardian was delighted. Soon afterwards he selected eight Friars for the Sierra Gorda missions, including Padre Serra and Padre Palou. Because the work there could not wait, he decided to shorten the time of preparation, which was ordinarily one year.

Before the volunteers left on their assignment, the Father Guardian called them together to instruct them once more. He gave them a final word of warning.

"It is only fair to tell you that this will be most difficult work. We have had a great deal of trouble with the Pames. Also, the climate can be most uncomfortable. Many of our missionaries have lost their health in the Sierra Gorda."

Father Guardian continued to speak, but Padre Serra hardly heard him. Nothing he could say would dampen the little Friar's spirits.

"At last," he thought. "At last, this is the moment for which I have waited and prayed. And, best of all, Francisco is to be my companion in this work, too. It is almost too much."

In a few days Padre Serra with Padre Palou set out on their journey. Again it was a long walk — about two hundred miles to the north. And still it was only the beginning.

Chapter Five

The women were amused to see the nearsighted little Friar trying to thread a needle.

V . . . . The Little Missionary of Sierra Gorda

THE missions of Sierra Gorda were made up of little more than five wooden churches each separated from its neighbor by a few miles of rugged terrain. The missions were nestled in a group of tall mountains north of Mexico City. The climate here was hot and very humid. It was most unpleasant.

The soldiers attached to the military guard disliked their assignment. They were forever complaining about something. Now the headquarters of Jalpan was buzzing with the news that a new spiritual leader had been appointed.

"What can they be thinking of?" asked one soldier of his companion. "It must be quite clear by now that these Indians cannot be properly civilized. The good Padres have tried for almost six years to establish communities and teach the Christian way of life. And what has been accomplished? The Pames continue to kill and steal, and they run off to their own pagan God whenever they need something really important."

The other soldier nodded agreement. He sighed lazily. "As for myself, I sincerely wish that every one of them would disappear into the mountains and never come back. Then maybe this Padre Serra would give up and we could return to civilization once and for all."

The soldiers had not counted on Padre Serra's determination. Although the situation at Jalpan was discouraging, he had no intention of giving up.

"It is true that the converts do not come to the sacraments and many of them continue to worship their own God. It is also true that the Pames are poor workers and would rather steal than farm for their food. But with God's help we can change all this," he told Padre Palou cheerfully.

Padre Serra spent many long hours learning to speak the Pame language. It was hard to learn, but little by little he mastered it. He even wrote a little catechism in the Pame language to make things easier for the Indians.

At first it was only the children who showed signs of interest and friendliness. They were delighted by the little lame Friar who made up games and played with them. They loved the beautiful stories he told, too.

It was because of one of the stories that the children and Padre Serra began to plan a surprise for Christmas. The little Indian boys and girls were very excited.

At the mission center of Jalpan the Indian children came every day to study with their new friend.

Although their parents were still reluctant to become too friendly with the Friars, the children eagerly crowded about Padre Serra. Some leaned against his arm while he taught them. One little boy, the youngest of the group, insisted upon climbing into his lap.

"Work comes before play, children," Padre Serra had told them. "First we must study and then get to our little surprise."

Usually the children willingly did whatever the Padre asked. But today they were very restless. Little Juan, who had climbed into Padre Serra's lap, wriggled and fidgeted. It seemed like a very long lesson today. Juan was really too young to be a member of this class, but he liked to be near the Padre.

What he really enjoyed was the surprise they were planning. For on Christmas day the children were going to put on a play. It was, Juan knew, about some people with wings who came to show the shepherds a newborn baby.

Juan played the part of the smallest shepherd, who brought a tiny lambkin to the baby called Jesus. He especially liked this part because Padre Serra had told him that as a boy he had often taken care of the sheep. Thinking about the play made Juan more eager than ever to begin.

He wriggled about and looked directly into the Padre's eyes. "Is it time to begin practice now?" he asked hopefully.

The Padre smiled kindly. "No, not yet. It won't be long now. You must be patient, Juan," he said gently and then went on with the lesson.

Little Juan was disappointed, but he smiled fondly at his friend. He leaned his head happily against the Friar's shoulder and prepared to wait longer. He liked it when the Padre called him by name. It was the Padre who had given him this new name.

A few minutes passed but they seemed like hours to Juan. His eyes fell on the catechism from which Padre Serra was reading. Juan had an idea.

"If he can't read the book, he will have to stop," he thought. Suddenly he stretched out his little hands and covered the pages as best he could. He looked around shyly at the Padre from under his thick lashes.

The other children began to laugh. But Padre Serra was trying hard to look stern. "Juan," he chided gently, "if you cannot wait patiently, we will have to send you away until we are ready for you."

Poor Juan. He did not want to be sent away, but he was tired of waiting. Two large tears escaped from under his lashes. Now, he thought, the Padre is angry with me.

But Padre Serra was not really angry with Juan. He smiled a very understanding smile. "Well, our lesson today is a rather long one," he admitted. "Perhaps we had better finish it tomorrow."

The children were delighted. Now they could practice the play. Juan was so happy that he hugged the Padre. Amid shouts and laughter they all went off to work on the Christmas surprise.

There were several different classes taught at the mission each day. And so there were special classes for grown-ups, older children and the little ones. Men and women were probably taught separately, as was the custom.

The Indians had begun to trust the Friars more. They noticed that under the missionaries' direction the crops brought large harvests. It was a very happy Padre Palou who reported to his friend one day. A group of Indians had come to him asking for directions in the care and planting of the new crops. He was very excited.

"Think how much confidence they are showing in coming and asking our advice. Before, when we gave suggestions they were not always welcome."

Padre Serra was very pleased. "Francisco, I would never have believed how happy this work would make me. Even in our university days I did not realize how wonderful it would be."

His work continued to make him very happy and it went well. The surprise play at Christmas was a great success. Now for the very first time some of the Indians who had found it difficult to understand the lessons given by the missionaries, truly realized the meaning of the birth of Jesus. To the others it made the story beautifully clear.

After that there were other plays and processions on special feast days. These the Indians loved, for they were used to ceremonies. The church at Jalpan was always kept beautifully decorated. More and more of the Pames began to come to Mass.

Besides farming and catechism, the Pames learned new crafts and trades. The women learned to weave, spin and sew. Sometimes Padre Serra taught these lessons himself. The women were amused to see the nearsighted little Friar trying to thread a needle.

Gradually the Indians became used to working each day. At first it had been difficult to get them to do anything useful, for they had lived very lazily before the missionaries came. Padre Serra and the other Friars had to teach them that work is an important part of the Christian way of life. The Friar was always careful to reward those who showed special diligence. At last he decided that the men were ready for a very special project. One day he called them together before the little wooden church.

"My children, your hard work and devotion these past months have made me very happy. Our mission is growing very fast, and more and more of you are coming to our little church." He turned then, gesturing towards the small, weather-beaten structure.

"But see how small it is! There is hardly enough room for all of us inside."

The Indians agreed. They began to whisper excitedly among themselves. Finally one of them spoke aloud. "Padre, we could build another church. We can get more wood. We can make one bigger than this."

Padre Serra smiled. He was pleased by their interest and delighted that they should offer to do this work themselves. But a wooden church was not what he had in mind.

"Why not a church of stone?" he asked. "We have all the stone we will need here. Such a church will last many more years. It will be a fitting house for God."

Then Padre Serra showed the Indians the plans he had been working on. They gasped in amazement. The church looked so big. It was to be fifty-three yards long and eleven yards wide. It was to have a dome, a sacristy, a chapel and a tall bell tower.

Some of the Indians did not believe that it would be possible to build such a structure. Padre Serra only smiled confidently.

"It will take a long time, but we can do it," he promised them. "Shall we try?"

The Indians were very enthusiastic. They quickly learned to help the masons and carpenters. They hauled rocks and sand from the surrounding area, making the lime and mortar themselves. Padre Serra worked harder than anybody else. He carried stones and supervised all the work. Slowly, very slowly, the church took shape. It was seven long years before it was completed.

How proud the Indians were of their work! From the outside it was an imposing and beautiful structure. The bell tower rose high in the mountain air pointing towards heaven. The walls were well made and as solid as a fortress. Inside, the walls were adorned with statues and gilded altars. Today this splendid church is still in use, nearly two hundred years after it was built.

The missionaries of the other four churches of Sierra Gorda were inspired by Padre Serra's work and built similar churches. One of these missionaries was Padre Juan Crespi. Just as he had promised, he had joined his friends in their missionary work in the New World. Now he was assigned to work at Tilaco in the Sierra Gorda. His church there was beautiful, though it was smaller than Padre Serra's.

As soon as he could, Padre Serra had an organ installed in the new church. Some of the Indians were taught to play it. He was very happy about this. All along, the priests had been trying to teach the Indians to sing. It was a difficult and discouraging task. But it was even more difficult to discourage Padre Serra.

One method he found most valuable in teaching the Indians about the Catholic religion was dramatization. The Christmas plays were most successful. During Lent the events of the last days of Our Lord's life were also depicted.

Padre Serra had a Calvary chapel built on a high hill. This could easily be seen from the church. On each Friday during the Lenten season Padre Serra carried a large cross and made the Stations of the Cross along the way to this chapel. The Indians in procession joined him, and this was a very impressive ceremony.

Padre Palou was astonished by his friend's strength. Once he had tried to lift this cross himself. He stumbled and nearly fell. He told Padre Serra about this.

"It is remarkable, Padre. I am younger and certainly stronger than you and still I do not think I could carry this cross. How can you bear the weight?"

But Padre Serra only smiled. "It is not so heavy when we remember how our sins must burden the divine Saviour."

The little missionary was to spend more than eight years in the Sierra Gorda. As time went on, only one thing about the Pames really bothered him. Some of the Indians still visited their pagan god. This was Cachum, Mother of the Sun.

High in the mountains, reached by a narrow stone stairway, was the temple of the god. It was watched over by an old, old Indian. Inside the rough wooden building was the idol carved from stone. It was the image of a woman's face, carved from transparent white marble. Here many of the Pames still came to ask special favors — recovery from illness, relief from drought, and other necessities. Here, too, they presented themselves when they wished to be married. The moment they gave a sheet of paper — the marriage petition — into the hands of the old Indian caretaker, they considered themselves wed.

At last Padre Serra decided to question some young Christians about this. "You must realize that you cannot really be Christians until you promise to give up all others but the one true God."

As he spoke the new Christians became more and more uncomfortable. They had not realized how wrong they had been to go to Cachum. "You must decide between Cachum and the true God," Padre Serra told them gravely.

For several days these young men and women were not seen at the mission. Padre Serra was very worried. He hoped he had not driven them away. He spent a great deal of time in the church praying for them.

Then one day a murmur of excitement swept through the mission. Indians from the fields came running. Classes stopped. A strange and solemn procession was approaching. Padre Palou sent one of the children to the church for Padre Serra. In a moment he appeared on the steps.

As the procession drew nearer the assembled Pames gasped in amazement. For a small group of men were bearing a marble image on their shoulders. It was Cachum, their pagan god.

With tears in his eyes, Padre Serra stood on the church steps, silently thanking God. The men approached and presented the Padre with the image.

"We have chosen, Padre," they said. "None of our tribe will visit Cachum again." Padre Serra was so happy he could not speak. Later, on a trip back to Mexico City, he carried the image to the College of San Fernando as a reminder of the great works God performs through His love.

As President of the missions Padre Serra was often required to travel to the other four churches and oversee the work of his missionaries. These were long, hard journeys on foot, and they were dangerous. The way was rough and strange animals dwelt in the mountains. There was always the possibility of getting lost.

Padre Serra had worked with the Pames more than eight years when he was recalled to the College of San Fernando. Although he was sorry to leave his missions at Sierra Gorda he was delighted with the proposed new assignment. Both he and Padre Palou were to be sent by the College of San Fernando to help with the establishment of missions along the San Saba River in Texas. Here they were to work with the Indians of the Apache nation.

These Indians were extremely warlike. The Viceroy had already sent one hundred soldiers to establish a presidio to protect the missions. And nearby several missionaries from the College of Santa Cruz at Queretaro, Mexico, had built a mission. Two other missionaries from San Fernando had been sent ahead of Padre Palou and Padre Serra.

While the two friends waited at the College to be sent on their new assignment, terrible news was received from the new mission on the San Saba River. The Indians had attacked, killing the missionaries and many soldiers. Only one, Padre Molina, escaped.

Because of this, plans to establish the missions in Texas were postponed. The Viceroy had hoped to send out soldiers to punish the Indians, but for a long time nothing was done.

Padre Serra was disappointed that he could not at present work with the Apache Indians, but he waited patiently. He was always happy to do any work that God sent him. Meanwhile he helped train young Franciscans at the College of San Fernando and performed various other duties there. Like the other priests at the College, Padre Serra was often sent to towns near Mexico City to preach missions. This he did gladly.

The towns were often far apart and the journeys were very difficult. The Friars endured many hardships. Fortunately, though, people were kind and they could always find shelter in houses along the way. Once, on such a journey, Padre Serra and his companion had been planning to reach a town by nightfall. But instead they found themselves in open fields without a house in sight. They had not eaten since early morning and they were hungry and very thirsty.

His young companion looked at Padre Serra with mournful eyes. "Perhaps if we wait where we are, some travelers will find us?" he suggested halfheartedly.

"I'm afraid there is not much hope of that," replied Padre Serra. "This is hardly a well-traveled route. I am afraid that we will just have to spend the night in the open."

Suddenly his companion became very excited. "Padre, look!" he cried pointing ahead.

To his amazement Padre Serra could just make out a tiny hut in the distance near the roadway. He was very tired and his leg bothered him terribly. It would be difficult for him to go even that short distance. But he was thankful that they would find shelter. Slowly and painfully he and his companion walked to the hut. A bright light glowed in the window and a tall man in a long robe greeted them at the door.

"Welcome, friends," he said. "You must be tired and hungry. My wife will bring you some food and drink. Mary!" he called over his shoulder.

At once a lovely young woman came forward. Her eyes were kind and gentle. "Sit down, please," she begged. "Help yourselves," she offered, setting bowls of food before the grateful Friars.

Then, going to the end of the room, she brought back a beautiful baby, whom she held on her lap while seating herself at one end of the table. Her husband stood beside her.

Padre Serra could not take his eyes from the child. He had a strong feeling of love and perfect peace as he looked at the infant. The last thing he remembered before he fell asleep in the hut that night was the child's tiny hands held out towards the Friars. Then he knew no more till daylight.

The next morning the missionaries felt very refreshed. They thanked their hosts and went on their way. But along the road they met some muleteers.

The men asked the missionaries where they had spent the night. Padre Serra told them. The muleteers were amazed. "I know this area very well," said one of the men. "There is no such dwelling here."

"That is right," another joined in. "Along the entire route you traveled yesterday there is no house or ranch."

It was then that Padre Serra knew that what he had suspected was true. He fell to his knees and gave thanks to God. For he believed that the Heavenly Father had permitted the missionaries a vision of the Holy Family.

In Mexico City itself Padre Serra gained a splendid reputation. He preached often at the Cathedral. Soon the citizens came to know and love Padre Serra. He spoke simply and in terms they understood. But just at first they resented him.

Mexico City had many lazy and wealthy inhabitants who thought of little else but their own amusement. Padre Serra was shocked and saddened to learn that the ladies insisted upon having hot chocolate served to them in church after Mass. He thought that this way of life was wrong and he said so.

"Be careful," the other priests told him. "These people are very sensitive. If you insult them, they will not come to church any more."

"If they listen only to what they want to hear, let them go somewhere else. I will continue to speak the truth."

But there were some who could not listen to the truth. Once when Padre Serra was giving a mission to Catholics in a town outside Mexico City a very strange thing happened.

At Mass Padre Serra began to feel very strange after having drunk the wine that had been changed into the Blood of Our Lord. He suddenly found himself unable to form the words of the Mass prayers. He turned pale and was about to fall to the floor when one of the Friars ran up and caught him. Other priests rushed forward at once and carried him to the sacristy.

"What can it be?" they whispered, frightened. "He was fine only a little while ago."

When Padre Serra was able to speak, he told them what had happened. Many believed that the altar wine had been poisoned. An antidote was prepared and brought to him, but he would not drink it. He could not bring himself to take this after having consumed the Body and Blood of Our Lord.

"Don't worry," he told his friends. "All will be well." In a few hours he had indeed completely recovered, and went back to church to hear confessions.

News of this incident and of Padre Serra's remarkable recovery traveled quickly. Wherever Padre Serra was sent, crowds flocked to hear him speak. As a result many Christians turned away from sin, and the missions Padre Serra gave produced great spiritual benefits.

For more than eight years Padre Serra worked zealously at the many tasks assigned him at the College of San Fernando. But he continued to hope that one day he would be sent to the missions on the San Saba River. Instead, after several years he with Padre Palou received a different and unexpected appointment.

The missions on the peninsula of Baja or Lower California — a strip of land which today belongs to Mexico — had been established only at the cost of great hardship. During the early years two missionaries had met martyrdom there. Up to 1767, these missions had been under the direction of Jesuit priests, but now the Franciscans were being sent to replace the Jesuits. The College of San Fernando was asked for twelve missionaries. Even though the College was shorthanded, the Father Guardian was able to gather together the necessary group of Friars. Padre Serra was given the important task of heading this group.

So it was that in July of 1767 Padre Serra and Padre Palou set out with others on the long journey across Mexico to the Gulf of California. At the inland town of Tepic they waited until they were joined by additional missionaries, for it had been discovered after they set out that more than twelve Friars would be needed.

Padre Serra and Padre Palou rejoiced to find Padre Juan Crespi among the newcomers who were going to California with them. At last the whole group of Friars sailed from the port of San Blas on the mainland of Mexico, crossed the Gulf, and arrived at Loreto. This was the oldest and most important of the missions on the Lower California peninsula. It was Holy Saturday, April 2, 1768, when the Friars disembarked. Delays and stopovers had slowed the journey. It had been nine months between the time they left Mexico City and the day they arrived in Lower California.

There were fifteen missions to be cared for. Padre Serra appointed one of his missionaries to each. He sent Padre Palou to Mission San Francisco Xavier and Padre Crespi to Mission Purisima Concepcion. As Loreto was the largest, and the central mission, he stayed there himself with Padre Parron as his companion.

Padre Serra could see at once that he had his work cut out for him. While the Indians were waiting for the new missionaries to arrive, many had run away from the soldiers in charge of them. They stole whenever they could. It was going to be very difficult to get them to come back. While Padre Serra was working in the missions on the peninsula, plans were being made in Spain and in Mexico City that were to change his entire life.

In Spain alarming news had reached the ears of the King.

"Russian ships have been sighted along the coast above Alta California," his advisers told him. "There is the possibility that the Russians are thinking of coming down from the northwest to colonize California."

For some time Russians had been coasting along the American mainland seeking the valuable sea otter. Now, it was known, they were busily engaged in trade in what is today Alaska. Soon, no doubt, they would have permanent settlements there, and if they colonized Alta California first, this fine land might be lost to Spain forever.

As early as 1602, a Spanish explorer, Sebastian Vizcaino, had anchored at a port in Alta or Upper California which he called Monterey, meaning "the King's Hill." He had claimed the land for Spain. Now that claim was being threatened. Spain would have to move quickly to protect her lands in what is now the state of California. Orders were sent from Spain to the Viceroy in Mexico City. This was the Marques de Croix. He and the Inspector General, Jose de Galvez, made plans to occupy Upper California.

"We will send two ships," directed the Viceroy. "These will carry men and supplies to establish forts and settlements to prevent the Russians from coming farther south. The ships can find the Bay of Monterey, which Vizcaino claimed for Spain so long ago."

It was Jose de Galvez who suggested that a land expedition, also made up of two parts, be sent as well. Gaspar de Portola, an experienced soldier and newly appointed Governor of the two Californias, would be sent as military leader.

"We can send more men this way, and in a short time greatly strengthen our claim to California," he argued. "First the Padres can establish a mission for the Indians at San Diego. After the ships have left their supplies for the mission at this southernmost port and have met the land party, all who are not needed at San Diego can go on to seek Monterey. I have heard of just the man to be spiritual leader of such a difficult venture. His Superiors will permit him to go, I am sure. He is Padre Junipero Serra."

And so it was that Padre Serra received an urgent message to meet Galvez at Santa Ana, the Inspector General's headquarters in Lower California. Together they would work out the details of this plan.

How surprised Padre Serra was to learn that he had been chosen Father President of all the new missions to be established in Upper California. He was overwhelmed by this appointment. What a marvelous opportunity this was! He was to be God's pioneer in an unknown land.

Chapter Six

"Well, you are very slow today," boomed the mocking voice of a robust Spaniard nearby.

VI . . . . . . The Muleteer's Remedy

IN THE harbor of La Paz in the Lower California peninsula a ship rode at anchor. This was the *San Carlos,* which would leave in a few days and meet the two sections of the land expedition at San Diego in Upper California. Later the *San Antonio* would set sail from Cape San Lucas. The ships would bring necessary supplies for the new settlements. With the expedition divided into various parts, there was less chance of failure. Should misfortune befall one or more sections, at least some would arrive at the goal.

Captain Rivera had been chosen to lead the first land party. Commandant Portola, Governor of California, would lead the second part of the land expedition himself. It was with this latter group that Padre Serra, the Father President, would travel.

With habit tucked up about his legs, Padre Serra worked feverishly to complete the packing of equipment needed for the missions which would be founded in little known Upper California. Vestments, chalices and other religious articles were to be taken to the new missions from the abundant supplies already in Lower California.

"Well, you are very slow today," boomed the mocking voice of a robust Spaniard nearby.

This was obviously a fine gentleman who had shed his coat and rolled up his lace-trimmed sleeves to help with the packing. "If you carry on like this, the ships will never leave."

Padre Serra smiled goodnaturedly at Don Jose de Galvez. "Never fear, sir. I can keep up with you. Just take care that you pack those vestments carefully. We will want them fit for use when we open the mission of San Buenaventura."

At first the antics of the little Friar and the Inspector General caused much comment from the surprised soldiers who were also preparing for the journey. But now they had become used to it. That is, as much as possible, when one remembered that it was the Father President of the missions and the famous Jose de Galvez himself, whom the King had appointed to organize the expedition to Upper California, who were playing this little game. They were racing to see which could wrap and pack faster for a mission. Don Jose was arranging the vestments and all the other things needed for San Buenaventura, one of the future missions in which he was especially interested.

So far it had definitely been decided to establish three missions. San Diego, the first, would be founded at that harbor, where other Spanish ships had docked before. Then would come San Buenaventura to the north and even farther up the coast, Monterey. The entire expedition had been put under the patronage of St. Joseph, in honor of the Patron saint of Jose de Galvez.

In time, Padre Serra hoped, there would be a chain of missions lying along the coast of Upper California. In Spanish he called it *El Camino Real* — the Royal Highway. He thought of it as a kind of Golden Highway dedicated to the King of kings.

Padre Serra was happy with his great plans for this new land. He paused a moment in his work. "You know, I have been thinking," he told his companion.

"Well, what is it?" inquired Galvez, without stopping. "Don't think you can get me to waste time while I listen. I intend to win this race."

Padre Serra hesitated thoughtfully. "It is just that so many fine saints have been mentioned as patrons of our missions. But what of St. Francis, the founder of our Order? Isn't he to have a mission?"

Galvez grunted. "Humph! If St. Francis wants a mission, let him show us the place. Perhaps he can even find us another bay like Monterey," he answered in his decisive manner.

Monterey Bay had been discovered many years before by the Spanish explorer Vizcaino. He had described its beauty at great length. It was this bay that Commandant Portola was commissioned to find again after leading the missionaries to San Diego.

"In that case," said Padre Serra contentedly, "I am sure St. Francis will lead us to such a bay."

He was delighted with this new assignment. It was more than he had ever hoped for. He could not help grinning now at the serious way in which the Inspector General was attacking the job of packing. It had become clear to him that Galvez with his strong arms and superhuman efforts was winning the race easily.

The *San Carlos* was the first to sail, leaving on January 11, 1769. The following month the *San Antonio* left. The first part of the land expedition, under Captain Rivera, left on March 24. Padre Juan Crespi was with this group. He was very happy that he would be associated with Padre Serra in this new and important work. Portola and Padre Serra with the second land party were to leave a few weeks later. In time they would all meet at San Diego.

As Padre Serra traveled northward saying good-by to his friends at the various missions along the way, he came at last to that of San Francisco Xavier, where he spent a few last days with Padre Palou, who was to remain behind in Serra's place as head of the missions in Lower California.

Padre Palou was worried to see his friend looking so tired. Besides this, his limp was more pronounced than ever. He knew that the journey over the rugged coastal mountains would be a hard and dangerous one for a man of his years.

"I wish you could stay here and that I could make this journey for you," said Padre Palou sympathetically.

Padre Serra shook his head. He was much older now than when they had first reached the New World, almost fifty-six. Yet his eyes burned with an eager, young enthusiasm.

"When will you learn, Francisco? This is what I have dreamed of. Perhaps I look tired now because of all the extra work of preparation, but a few nights' rest will take care of that. Somehow I feel as though my life's work were just beginning. God has prepared for me tasks which are more important than anything I have ever done. I think I am happier now than I have ever been. And stronger, too," he added, hoping to allay his friend's fears.

Padre Palou could not help worrying. When he said good-by it was with tears in his eyes.

"I pray it will not be too long before we meet in Monterey to labor together in that vineyard," Father Serra said in parting. *"Vaya con Dios."*

But Padre Palou was not to be consoled. "Until we meet in eternity," he replied. He did not believe that his friend could survive the hardships of the long journey.

At the little mission of Guadalupe in Lower California, the Padre who was in charge had a surprise waiting.

"I think I have a very valuable companion for you," he said happily, leading a young Indian boy by the hand. The boy was small but sturdy. He looked up at Padre Serra shyly.

"This is Jose. He is a good boy. He speaks Spanish as well as several Indian dialects and is very eager for adventure. He would like to go with you. He has been trained by us for many useful services."

"This is indeed a pleasant surprise," replied Padre Serra kindly. "But he must be very young. How old are you, Jose?"

"I am fifteen," answered the boy politely.

"Fifteen!" exclaimed the Friar. "I would have guessed ten from your size." And then he had to laugh, remembering the problems he had had because of his size when he was fifteen.

Jose looked apprehensive. He was sure that the Padre would not want him now. "He must be laughing because it is foolish to think that one so small could be of any help," he thought unhappily. He was trying to fight back the tears that stung his eyes.

But now the Padre was holding out his hand. He spoke in the most understanding tone.

"You know, Jose, I have the very distinct feeling that before long you will find yourself growing very tall. I will be very happy to have you as my friend, companion and helper."

Right then and there Jose decided that he would learn to love the Padre. The next day they set out early. When the boy grew tired Padre Serra insisted that he ride on the mule that carried one of the mission bells. But the Friar himself always walked. His sandals made a soft, uneven sound on the pathway, for he was limping badly.

At Velicata they found Commandant Portola and the second part of the land expedition ready and waiting for them. While Padre Serra was there, he founded a new mission, leaving Father Miguel de la Campa in charge as the others started out for unknown lands.

In the morning after Mass and Holy Communion for the entire company, the expedition set out. Jose was very excited. He tried to stay close to Padre Serra. But now and then he just had to run on ahead to see what was coming next. Besides, it seemed to him that the Padre was very slow. His leg seemed to be bothering him more than ever. Sometimes Jose would run to the side of the trail and come back, his eyes shining.

"Padre, Padre! Wait till you see the deer. They are feeding close by and not at all afraid. I almost touched one," he would cry.

And the Padre would smile. "That's fine, Jose, and what else do you see?"

Then the boy would be off again. "Rabbits," he would call. "They're all around. Take care not to step on one." Each night before retiring, Padre Serra wrote the day's events in a little book. Jose, who was very tired at the end of the day, had all he could do to keep from falling asleep over his evening meal.

"More work, Padre?" he asked, drowsily watching the Friar. "What is it you are writing?"

"This is a diary," came the reply. "We are among the first Spaniards to travel over this land. It is a good idea to keep a record so that others who follow may know more of this part of the world."

But Jose had closed his eyes and was fast asleep before Padre Serra had finished speaking.

The next night Jose found himself wide awake after the rest were asleep. Something was wrong with the Padre. The boy was sure that it was very painful for him to walk at all. Many times he had begged the Padre to ride the little mule, but in vain. Now the brave little Friar was lying nearly helpless on the ground. It was difficult for him even to sit up. Some of the soldiers had reported this to Commandant Portola. Jose saw the big man coming towards them.

The Commandant was brisk, and a note of annoyance rang in his voice. "Now, what is this?" he addressed himself to the helpless Friar. "I knew, I just knew it," he said shaking his head disgustedly. "I told Galvez that a lame Friar would only cause trouble. And I see I was right. Well, well."

The Commandant spoke rapidly because he was confused and did not know what to do. If he went on without the Friar, he would lose the services of this fine spiritual leader. If he allowed him to continue the journey, the whole expedition might be slowed up because of the presence of an invalid. And though the Commandant would not admit it, there was something about this small priest with the determined spirit that fascinated him. He had come to like the Padre.

He made his decision. "I am sending you back to San Fernando at Velicata with some of my men tomorrow." He waved the Padre's protests aside, not wanting to get into a discussion with this persuasive man. "These are my orders. There is nothing to be said." He turned to go, and the Padre called after him in his firm, clear voice, "It may be that it is not God's will that I reach San Diego, although I pray He will give me the strength. Even though I may die on the way, I will not turn back."

Commandant Portola came back slowly. This was a most remarkable man, he was thinking. He never failed to be amazed by the little Padre's courage.

The ring of annoyance left his voice. He spoke gently, for he was certain that the Padre would not survive the difficult journey. "Very well, if that is your wish. I will have a litter made. The Indians can carry you for the rest of the journey." Once again he turned to go.

But Padre Serra was distressed at the thought of the added hardship this would cause the Christian Indians who were accompanying them.

The priest looked up at the clear sky. He had to bite his lip to hold back the cries of pain. He mustn't wake Jose. The boy had finally fallen asleep. Nearby a muleteer busily worked among his charges. He whistled softly to himself. He was a cheerful, good-natured fellow and Padre Serra liked him. Now he called to him softly.

"Juan, Juan. Can you come here a moment?"

"Certainly, Padre. How are you feeling? Can I do something for you?"

"Yes, Juan." It was a painful effort for the Padre to speak. "Surely you must have a remedy for your mules when they have a leg infection."

The muleteer was puzzled. "Why, yes, Padre. I make a hot poultice and apply it to the wound. It is very painful, but mules are able to bear that sort of thing. It is usually successful."

Padre Serra touched the muleteer's hand. "Well, Juan. Would you pretend that I am one of your mules?" And he drew back his habit to reveal the infected place on his leg.

Juan gasped. "But, Padre, you can't mean it. The remedy is for animals. It would be much too painful. I couldn't."

The Padre wouldn't listen. "Please, Juan. I need your help. I must be ready to go on with the expedition tomorrow."

After much pleading the old muleteer consented. His hands trembled as he worked. He was amazed at the way the little missionary bore the pain without making a sound. He could not stop the tears that flowed in sympathy from his own eyes. Padre Serra lay very still, his lips moving steadily in prayer. At last he slept.

The next day dawned bright and rosy. The men roused slowly and prepared for another hard trip. Padre Serra opened his eyes to find little Jose bending over him.

"The men are making a litter to carry you," he said sadly. Padre Serra sat up slowly. He felt much better. Soon he was standing beside Jose. His leg was very much improved. Juan came over anxiously watching the Padre.

"I cannot thank you enough, Juan," Padre Serra told the muleteer. "I am sure I will be able to carry on with my journey now."

At that moment Commandant Portola came up. He could not believe his eyes when he saw Padre Serra standing smiling before him. Portola did not know what to say. He was amazed. "I — I am glad, of course," he stammered at last. Then he walked quietly away.

Padre Serra bowed his head. "Whatever you say, Commandant," he agreed quietly.

The incident had truly impressed the Commandant. He thought of it many times that day, not knowing what to make of it. Finally he turned to his Sergeant.

"This is a very remarkable priest," he said. "Very remarkable indeed."

Chapter Seven

"Padre, Padre! Look!" cried Jose excitedly. "Horsemen! I see soldiers!"

VII . . . . Sergeant Ortega's Courage

THE journey up the peninsula to Alta California was very difficult. The trails were rough, and much of the land was desert. The farther they went the more Jose wondered why he had ever thought pioneering would be so exciting. It seemed to him that one day was very like all the others.

In the morning, before starting, he would serve Mass for Padre Serra. Then they would travel doggedly on. When evening came he was glad to rest, only to start the whole thing over again.

The Friars greeted each new day happily. Padre Serra was always especially cheerful. For some time now the Friars had been engaged in what Jose thought was a foolish occupation.

"We must give names to the places we pass — lakes, streams and any important landmarks," Padre Serra had told his fellow Friars. It all seemed very silly to Jose, and he questioned the Padre about it.

"Why do you bother, Padre? You give the places one name and the soldiers who are making maps give them another. It all seems very confused."

This was very true. The Friars named various places after saints and prominent Spanish figures of whom they were reminded. But the soldiers named them after incidents that had occurred there. Once a soldier shot down a seagull and they called that place *Gaviota* Pass. A place where a lame Indian was seen was called *El Cojo* and so on.

But Padre Serra only smiled. "Well, Jose," he said, "it is better to have too many names instead of no name at all."

Everyone had been prepared for danger and hardships, but when the Indians appeared the soldiers hardly knew what to do. The first Indians they saw were hostile, and Portola finally ordered shots fired into the air to frighten them and keep them from attacking.

Then one evening as the groups were making camp, some Indians appeared on the hillside. "I count ten men, and those two would appear to be boys," Sergeant Ortega whispered. They were all surprised to find that these Indians wore nothing at all.

"We'd better be careful since we don't know how many may be lurking near by. If they are unfriendly, this could be a disaster," the Commandant reminded the Sergeant.

While they waited Padre Serra had gone into action. He took aside Jose and another Indian who was traveling with the Spaniards. They might be able to act as interpreters. He gave them figs and meat for the unexpected visitors.

"Tell them we are friends," he said. "Ask them to come and meet us."

While everyone watched, Jose and the interpreter went up to the Indians. Finally Jose returned, with good news. The Indians were friendly. "They say that they cannot come yet. They are waiting for a present to arrive which they want to give you, Padre."

Soon some messengers arrived, bringing with them a gift of cooked mescal. A little later two women appeared. Padre Serra was very glad to find that the ladies were modestly dressed, being completely covered with clothes of a heavy, rough material. One of the women was carrying a huge pancake of dough on her head. When Padre Serra blessed her, she placed the sticky object in his hand, much to everyone's amusement.

The next day they saw more of these Indians. Although Commandant Portola was relieved to find them friendly, he was disgusted by their childish behavior.

A large number of the Indians had decided to accompany the expedition for a little way. Once, as they were going down a difficult narrow road, the Indians made so much noise with their shouting that the mules and horses began to bolt. This delighted the Indians. Not realizing that they were doing any harm, they continued to amuse themselves in this way.

Portola was very annoyed. He was afraid that they would cause a stampede. The road was so treacherous that both animals and men might be killed. The soldiers and the Friars scolded the Indians, but they paid no attention. At last Portola had shots fired into the air and the Indians stopped.

Afterwards the Commandant approached Padre Serra. "Well, well, what do you think of your friendly Indians now, Padre?" he inquired disgustedly.

"They do not mean to be vicious. They just do not know any better," the priest replied softly.

But the Commandant walked off angrily. They Jose asked something that had been bothering him for some time. He had grown to love Padre Serra just as he knew he would. He did not like the way the Commandant spoke to his friend sometimes.

"Why is the Commandant always so angry? He doesn't seem to like anyone at all."

Padre Serra put his arm about the boy's shoulders. "You must not take Commandant Portola's gruff tones for dislike, Jose. He is a man with many responsibilities. All of us, even you and I, depend upon him as our military leader. I believe he speaks that way to hide his concern even from himself."

Once when Padre Serra was making friends with some Indians they pointed and giggled until the priest realized that his glasses were creating all the excitement. One of them seemed to want to examine the glasses more closely.

"So these interest you, do they?" he asked, taking them off. Without thinking, he handed them to the Indian to look at. In another minute the Indian had run away and the glasses were gone.

Padre Serra was astonished. This was something he had not expected. Here he was more than a thousand miles away from any place where glasses could be supplied. It might be a year before he could get new spectacles.

"Jose," he called urgently. Telling the boy what had happened, he said: "We must go after them and try to get the glasses back."

Jose's mouth fell open. "Padre, it would be hopeless. We don't even know where they have gone."

"Somehow we will manage. I must have my glasses."

Off they went, leaving the trail in pursuit of the Indians. Here and there they met other Indians and inquired about the spectacles, using signs without much success.

"We'd better give up, Padre. It is impossible to find them. Why, they could be miles from here by now the way these people pass things about. Let's go back," he pleaded.

But Padre Serra would not give up. And soon he was rewarded. Up ahead they could see two Indian women arguing. One had something on her head that caught the sun's rays. The other seemed to be making fun of this new ornament. As Padre Serra and Jose approached, they could see that these were the missing spectacles.

Jose and Padre paused. Here was another problem. "Will they give them back?" asked the boy uncertainly. "We must not start any trouble."

"I have an idea," said Padre Serra, drawing some colored beads from his habit. After many signs and some arguing the women agreed to exchange the glasses for the brighter necklaces.

Padre Serra was so relieved to get his spectacles back that he was able to joke with Jose about the way the women meant to use them. They returned to camp laughing, but the Padre was careful after that not to let his possessions leave him for a moment.

One morning Padre Serra was in an unusually happy frame of mind when he woke Jose.

"Padre, how can you be so cheerful?" the boy asked gloomily.

There was really very little to be cheerful about. They were traveling through a desert. The water supply was running low and, to make matters worse, it appeared that they might be lost.

"It seems to me," said Jose, "that things are going from bad to worse. Soon we will not be able to find any water, and then what will become of us? We will probably become food for the buzzards."

Jose knew that the Padre was disappointed in him, but he just couldn't help it. Padre Serra looked at him reproachfully. "We must never give up hope, my son. God is watching over us. Besides, today is a special occasion. It is the Feast of St. Anthony of Padua, the saint of many miracles. Perhaps he will show us the way out of our difficulties."

And, indeed, it did seem that the good saint was watching over them. That morning the scouts sent back word that they had found two water holes. The men were overjoyed.

"When we reach this place we will name it after the wonder-worker saint, our patron of this glorious day," they cried happily.

But when they did reach the water holes, the animals swarmed around them and drank all the water. There was hardly any left for cooking. The meal that evening, cooked without benefit of water, was worse than usual.

Jose was more discouraged than ever. "We should call this place San Antonio of the Hardships, I think," he told the Padre bitterly. Padre Serra was sorry about the disappointment, too. But he was still hopeful. And that evening he was rewarded once again.

There was much excitement when word again came from the scouts who had once more gone ahead of the party. The men shouted and threw their hats into the air. "Water, two beautiful streams only a day away!" came the news. "The desert is ended. Green, green pastures and water!"

Padre Serra turned to Jose. "What do you think of St. Anthony now?"

The boy was too ashamed to answer. The new lands were very beautiful. It was a delight just to look at trees and grass instead of parched sands. And still, their troubles were not over.

As soon as they reached pleasant land, some of the Indians who had come with them from Baja California began to desert. These Indians had been brought along to help with the building of the new missions.

"The other Indians say that they do not know why these men have disappeared. Maybe they were afraid of what is ahead," Jose told the Friars.

"It is too bad. We needed their assistance. Now we must pray for them — they will need God's in this unknown land," said Padre Serra.

But as time went on even the soldiers became discontented. They fought among themselves. Many whispered about deserting. They had traveled for several months, and still there were no signs to tell them that they were nearing San Diego. And now the journey became more difficult than ever. They made their way over rocky mountain trails. The cliffs fell away so sharply that they were constantly in danger of slipping and losing their lives.

Even Jose began to be resentful. He became more and more annoyed by the extra weight of the mission bell on the mule. It only made the climbing harder.

"We might as well leave it here," he thought angrily. "The Padre will probably never use it." He was careful to keep these thoughts to himself. But there was something about Padre Serra's eyes. The boy suspected that the little Friar knew what he was thinking. He was ashamed, but he could not drive the thoughts away.

The company slowed down considerably. They were unable to do more than crawl most of the time. At last the journey became so difficult that the men refused to go on.

"How do we know what is ahead? Perhaps we are hopelessly lost and will never find San Diego. Let us go back before it is too late," they begged.

Commandant Portola became very angry. He forced his men to go on, but he did not know how long he could control them. It was Sergeant Ortega who brought hope to the expedition. Courageously he volunteered to set out with another soldier and several Indians to see what lay ahead. They came to Padre Serra for a special blessing.

"You are very brave, my sons. *Vaya con Dios,* and bring back good news," he said, blessing them.

While Sergeant Ortega was gone, Commandant Portola forced his men forward. Everyone worried about the valiant soldier and his scouting party. No one dared say anything. But Sergeant Ortega did not fail them. Three days later they found a note from him, encouraging them to go onward. Considerably cheered, they pushed ahead.

Then, two days later, the party heard a voice from a hilltop. "Commandant, Commandant!" It was Sergeant Ortega returning with a report of what he had found. The company was delighted to see him. Padre Serra breathed a prayer of thanksgiving for Ortega's safe journey.

Everyone was heartened by the Sergeant's news. He had not yet sighted San Diego, but there were indications that it must be close by. With Portola's permission he took more supplies and set out again.

There was another week of difficult traveling. But the company was in high spirits now. The end of the journey was certainly near at hand. They even met an Indian wearing blue cloth with he said had been given him by Spaniards at San Diego. He told the soldiers that he had also seen men there dressed like Padre Serra.

On June 28 Sergeant Ortega returned again. This time the scouting party was not alone. "Padre, Padre! Look!" cried Jose excitedly. "Horsemen! I think — yes, they are soldiers!"

Everyone looked to the north. There, riding towards them, was Sergeant Ortega accompanied by ten Spanish soldiers. Ortega and his scouts had reached San Diego and found Rivera's group. They were bringing supplies and fresh animals to speed Portola's tired party on its way.

At once the company changed from a band of tired men to a group of wildly happy individuals. They rushed forward eagerly. Sergeant Ortega was the hero of the day!

For two more days the Sergeant led them onward. They went gladly now. At last, on July 1, 1769, they came to a place along the shore where the sea curved inland. It was the port of San Diego. There, riding at anchor, were the two ships. A few hours later they sighted Rivera's camp.

The men set up a tremendous noise with their shouts of joy. Padre Serra bent down and kissed the earth. A glorious song of praise filled his heart. He was very thankful that God had permitted them to reach their destination.

"Well, Padre," cried Jose, his eyes shining. "We will be using the mission bell after all."

Chapter Eight

"A sail, a sail!" they shouted. Only Padre Serra was silent; he fell to his knees and wept for joy.

VIII . . . . St. Joseph's Miracle

COMMANDANT Portola's gun salute boomed through the stillness. Shouts and cries of welcome reached the approaching land party. An answering salute echoed through the mountain walls. Soon members of Rivera's band were rushing to meet their valiant comrades. It was July 1, and for forty days Portola's party had been on the march from Velicata.

Padre Juan Crespi grasped the hands of his former teacher and greeted him with tears of joy.

"We worried. We prayed. And now you are here. Thanks be to God," he cried fervently.

After the happiness of seeing friends again came grim and dismal facts. Captain Rivera took Commandant Portola aside. "We have had a great deal of trouble. Our men are sick and dying. The Captain and crew of the *San Carlos,* except for one sailor and the cook, are dead from scurvy. The crew of the *San Antonio* are also suffering from this disease. Neither ship is in condition to go on to find Monterey. Besides this, our supplies are low."

Commandant Portola accepted this news in silence. He had thought that upon reaching San Diego his difficulties would be over. But the Commandant was a man of unusual strength and determination. He sighed heavily.

"Well, Captain, there is no point in dwelling on our misfortunes. We must be thankful for what we have. Today we will rest. Tomorrow we will decide what to do."

The next morning Padre Serra celebrated a Mass of thanksgiving. Then the leaders met to discuss the situation.

The Commandant laid the problems before them. "Many of our men are sick or dying. They must be taken care of. The mission must be established. We have not been able to send out a ship to search for Monterey. The Bay *must* be found. Now, what are we to do?"

Suggestions were made and discussed. At last the following plan was drawn up. Padre Serra, Padre Parron and Padre Vizcaino would remain at San Diego. They would be provided with a handful of soldiers. Here the sick would be nursed to health. The Friars who stayed behind would found the mission of San Diego.

As soon as a few men could be gathered together from among the healthy, the *San Antonio* would be sent back to Baja California. The ship could bring back fresh crews for herself and the *San Carlos* as well as desperately needed supplies. In the meantime Commandant Portola, with Captain Rivera and Padre Juan Crespi, would go north by land in search of the lost Monterey Bay.

The plan was put into action at once. Commandant Portola gathered his men and started forth on his expedition. The remaining soldiers set about the business of building huts and a kind of fence or palisade for protection. One of the huts was set aside to be used as a temporary church. Thus was the mission of San Diego begun.

"And now, Jose," Padre Serra told his young friend, "we will make use of the mission bell."

Jose watched eagerly as the Padres set up a large cross outdoors within sight of the sea. He helped wherever he was needed.

"What shall I do now?" he would ask.

"Why not begin gathering some boughs for the roof of the hut?" suggested Padre Vizcaino.

And Jose would run off as though there were wings on his feet. With the help of some of the soldiers he carried piles of branches from trees in the nearby woods. It wasn't long before the rough chapel was finished. At last all was ready.

"All right, Jose," said Padre Serra happily, "bring the bell."

Proudly the boy led the little mule that had carried both himself and the bell all the way from Baja (or Lower) California. Carefully the Friars hung the bell on the bough of a nearby tree. Now the Indians could come to the mission to learn about our Divine Lord.

At the end of the impressive ceremony Padre Serra began to ring the mission bell for the first time. The sound carried clearly through the morning air. It floated out over the harbor. It rang over the land and sounded far away in the hills and surrounding woods.

"Come!" cried Padre Serra, "Come, one and all, to learn of the glory of Christ."

There was a long silence. Jose looked about him carefully. Now the Indians would come. The Padre had called them. But when no one appeared, Jose was very disappointed.

"Where are they, Padre?" he asked later that day. "Didn't they hear you?"

"They heard, Jose, and they will come. They don't know what to make of us now, but they will come," replied the little Friar confidently.

Padre Serra was right. The Indians did come. Slow and timid at first, they soon swarmed about the new mission. They examined everything curiously. The huts, the chapel, the cross — all these interested them. They found the soldiers' uniforms and the Padres' clothing most interesting.

Padre Serra offered them food, but they would not take it. They did accept the beads and in return they hung strings of berries and fish on the cross, thinking that this must be the white man's God.

The first thing Padre Serra wanted to do was learn the Indians' dialect so that he could begin to teach them. He gathered together some of the men who came and began lessons.

The Indians took this as a kind of game. They howled with laughter as the Padre tried to pronounce the new words and phrases. Try as he would, Padre Serra did not seem to be getting anywhere. And soon he began to suspect the truth.

"They are just making fun of us," said Jose resentfully. "One day a word means one thing and the next day another. They don't want us to learn."

Padre Serra had to admit that Jose was probably right. The next day he asked him to gather together some little boys.

"Children are more direct and honest. Perhaps they will be more willing to help," he said.

After that the lessons went well. The priest began to learn the strange dialect, and to everyone's delight the boys began to pick up Spanish. Padre Serra taught them his favorite greeting, "*Amad a Dios* — Love God." Soon the Indians were making daily use of it.

"Now we are making progress," Padre Serra exclaimed happily. The boys were coming every morning to recite the simple prayers they had learned and to listen to the kindly Padre's stories. Little by little they were being taught to be Christians.

Padre Serra was pleased with these beginnings. But the soldiers did not trust the Indians. The latter knew little about guns and firearms and their deadly power. Thus they had little fear of them, as yet. Regularly they would prowl around the mission at night and steal whatever they could lay hands on. Even the sails of the one ship still in harbor were not safe from them.

"If only they would ask for what they need," said Padre Serra sadly, "we would give it to them."

These plunderings were nothing compared to what happened next. The Indians had been in the mission often enough to know exactly where everything was. They also knew that the small number of guards left by Commandant Portola did not make a strong barrier and that, of the rest of the Spaniards, some were sick and too weak for activity. The little things they had been able to steal here and there did not satisfy them. They wanted more. And they planned to get it.

On August 15 the Indians waited until Padre Parron had gone to the ship in the company of two soldiers. He was to say Mass there on this feast day of the Assumption.

This left only four soldiers to protect the mission. It seemed peaceful enough. Padre Serra celebrated Mass. Some of the Indians who were studying to become Christians, attended.

Then, without warning, a band of Indians swooped down upon the mission, screaming and shooting arrows. The handful of soldiers manned the guns. Padre Serra took in the situation at once. He, Padre Vizcaino and Jose fled to Padre Serra's hut for safety. A few others had reached there before them. Jose helped barricade the openings as best he could. All the while frenzied yells and shouts pierced the air. The mission was seriously threatened. The Spaniards were vastly outnumbered.

Jose's hands shook with terror as he helped the Padre pull a board across the last little opening. Padre Serra placed his hand on Jose's shoulder. There was love and understanding in his eyes. "All will be well, my son," he said kindly. "God is watching over us."

Jose straightened his shoulders resolutely. He knew that the soldiers were shorthanded and he could not bear to think of anything happening to the good Friars. He backed slowly towards the doorway.

"The soldiers will need someone to load the guns," he said. Before anyone could stop him the boy rushed outdoors, replacing the barricade as soon as he was on the outside. Padre Serra gasped in surprise. At that moment a surge of furious shouts and a shower of arrows rained down on the little hut. The Friars knelt in prayer.

Outside, the Indians swarmed about, firing arrows on the valiant band of defenders. Although the number of soldiers was so small, each time their guns fired the Indians fell back. They were terrified by these weapons. Soon realizing that arrows were no match for these deadly explosions, the Indians began to retreat.

As the sound of their shouting began to fade and die out Padre Vizcaino reached up, lifted the barricade, and peered out from behind the fiber curtain at the doorway. But the enemy had not yet surrendered. An arrow pierced the priest's hand.

Just then there was a strange, painful cry outside. Padre Serra recognized Jose's voice and ran to the doorway. His heart sank as the boy fell into his arms. An arrow had struck him in the throat. He managed a few words.

"Padre, give me absolution. The Indians have killed me." He collapsed. In a few minutes, with Padre Serra kneeling beside him, the boy died.

Suddenly every misfortune that had befallen seemed to bear heavily upon Padre Serra. The treachery of the Indians, the plight of the sick, concern about the delay in finding Monterey, the lack of needed supplies. And now Jose, his beloved little helper, had died at the hands of the very creatures he was trying to help. It was almost too much. Padre Serra could not stop the terrible sobs that shook his body.

The Indians were driven back. The soldiers had killed and wounded many of them. These tired Spaniards were terribly disgusted. They were sure that the Indians had turned hostile and would never return. They saw no point in continuing work on the mission when it would never be used to teach these pagans. They worked halfheartedly.

But the soldiers were wrong. Out of the tragedy came an unexpected victory. Indians, wounded by the soldiers' bullets, wandered into the camp for help. To the soldiers' disgust the priests welcomed them and nursed their wounds. The Indians were very grateful. At last they had begun to trust these white men. Once again they began to come regularly.

Padre Serra missed his friend Jose. He thought of him often. He felt sure that the boy was with Our Lord in heaven.

One of the Indian boys he was teaching now reminded him of Jose. He was a boy of about fifteen years, who came to instructions every day and learned quickly.

One day Padre Serra asked the boy if he could find a family who would allow the Friars to baptize their baby. He explained exactly what this meant so that the lad would understand. He wanted to be sure that the boy would know exactly what Baptism was.

The boy promised to see if he could find such a family. Padre Serra sighed wistfully. "If only we could have one Baptism — the first in this new land of Upper California, how wonderful it would be! It would be a beginning — a real beginning."

Very soon afterward the boy was able to keep his promise. He had found the family. When Padre Serra heard the news he was delighted.

"This is a glorious day for our little mission," he cried. "Our Lord must have guided you," he told the boy.

The Indian lad beamed with pleasure. The next day he stood proudly beside the priest while the Indian father, bearing a tiny baby in his arms, entered the chapel, followed closely by his friends and relatives. Everyone was very happy. The corporal of the guard acted as godfather to the child. The Indians seemed more and more impressed as the ceremony progressed.

But just as the Padre prepared to pour the water over the child's head, an excited murmur arose among the Indians. Suddenly they snatched the baby from the Friar's hands and rushed away with it.

Padre Serra was terribly disappointed. He restrained the soldiers from going after the Indians and punishing them.

"We must forgive them, after all. They do not know any better," he said. But there were tears in his eyes.

The missionaries were able to solve most of the difficulties at San Diego. But far to the north, the land expedition was searching frantically for the oval Bay of Monterey described by the explorer Vizcaino.

The men had not found the bay. Instead they had wandered unknowingly too far north. Here they made a very important discovery which they did not recognize at the time. Reaching a hilltop, some of the soldiers looked upon a magnificent sight. The waters of the Pacific sparkled brilliantly in the clear, clean air as they flowed majestically between a golden gateway of land on either side. To the north, the shore curved inland, forming a little cove. This we know today as Drake's Bay, which lies a little to the north of the city of San Francisco. But, alas, this was not what they were seeking.

Only Padre Crespi realized the significance of the spot. "Padre Serra said that St. Francis would find a place for his own mission and perhaps even a bay to go with it. Well, here it is," he thought. "San Francisco Bay!" He did not know that a larger and much more important bay lay to the east, and would one day bear this name.

Commandant Portola did not share Padre Crespi's enthusiasm. His men had come down with scurvy. They had wasted months in searching for something they would never find. It was hopeless, he decided. He turned his tired band about, trudging the five hundred and fifty miles back to San Diego. They arrived there January 24, 1770.

When Padre Serra informed the Commandant of all that had happened at the mission during his absence and the military leader learned that the *San Antonio* had not yet returned with the needed supplies and help, Portola was very discouraged. As the weeks went by and February gave way to March, and there was still no sign of the supply ship, he was forced to make a decision.

"We must return to Mexico," he said finally. "There is no point in this needless suffering any longer. We will never be able to tame these wild savages. As for Monterey — well, maps are uncertain; even history is uncertain. We cannot hope to find the bay now. We will have to admit defeat."

Padre Serra was stunned. "You can't mean this, Commandant," he cried, desperately hoping to change the Commandant's mind. "After all we have suffered, to give up now means that all who have died, have died for nothing. You have always been so courageous. We can't give up now."

But Commandant Portola was a stubborn man. He was certain that he had made the right decision. He would not change his mind.

"Very well; then leave me and the other Friars here. We will carry on the mission alone. Later you can send supplies and a new band of soldiers. We have just begun to make progress," the priest begged.

Commandant Portola rose angrily. "Of course you cannot stay here without protection. We are all leaving. These are my orders. You must obey them."

Still Padre Serra did not want to give up. He knew it would be many years before another attempt to establish these missions would be made. During all that time how many Indians would die without knowledge of Our Lord? He could not go. God would not want them to go.

At last he said, "As you say, Commandant. But grant me one more favor. In nine days it will be the Feast of St. Joseph, the patron of our mission. Let us make a novena. If the *San Antonio* does not come by then, I too will admit defeat. Please."

Padre Serra looked at the Commandant with steady eyes in which the light of faith burned brightly. Portola looked away. He thought that he had never seen such faith in anyone. He could not deny the Padre's wish.

"Very well," he agreed reluctantly, "but we cannot wait longer than that." For nine days the novena went on and still the ship did not come. By St. Joseph's Day the soldiers were packed and ready.

When evening came, Portola went to Padre Serra in the chapel. The Friar had prayed so hard and Portola knew how much San Diego meant to him. The Commandant was truly sorry that they had to go. But there was no reason to hope that the *San Antonio* would come now. He stood in the doorway, his hat in his hand. Padre Serra was no longer young. If he should have to leave San Diego he would not return. If a new expedition was organized in a few years, a younger man would be appointed President of the missions. This would be the end of the priest's dream, and Portola sympathized with him.

Padre Serra turned from the altar and saw Portola standing there. "Don't look so forlorn, Commandant," he whispered. "St. Joseph's Day is not yet over." But his voice did not ring with its former certainty.

Quietly he made his way to the band of hopeful men awaiting the sight of the *San Antonio.* Everyone was silent. That morning they had sung the Mass in honor of St. Joseph, thanking him for his intercession, without knowing whether or not their petition had been granted. Hour after hour they waited. The sun was going down and a rosy sunset tinted the sky. Then a dark fleck no bigger than a fly came into view. The men held their breath. Could it be? They waited a little longer. No, there could be no mistake.

"A sail, a sail!" they shouted. "A sail, a sail!" the cry was taken up and spread throughout the camp.

"The *San Antonio* has come! Praised be God!" cried the Friars.

"A miracle, a miracle!" exclaimed the men in awed voices.

Only Padre Serra was silent. He fell to his knees and wept for joy. He did not know whether it was actually a miracle. He was only sure it was an answer to prayer.

Chapter Nine

An altar was set up under an oak, . . . and Padre Serra sang Mass.

IX . . . . . . Padre Serra's Victory

WHAT a change the coming of the *San Antonio* brought about in the explorers and the missionaries! Only a day before, they had been in deep despair. And now their hearts were filled with hope and great expectations for the future.

Surely their tasks of exploration and founding settlements in the New World had been especially blessed. They fell to the work at hand with enthusiasm. Captain Perez of the *San Antonio* was certain that Monterey could be found.

"Vizcaino was a great explorer, but his map is over one hundred and fifty years old. By our standards it is probably most inaccurate. It seems to me that you must have overshot the mark," he told Portola confidently.

"Let us try again. I will sail up the coast and you can go by land. With both of us searching in that way, we cannot fail."

After the almost miraculous appearance of the *San Antonio,* Commandant Portola would hesitate to doubt anything again.

"Good. But I must ask that this time Padre Serra travel by sea. What do you say, Padre? It will give your leg a good rest. Perhaps it will heal altogether."

Padre Serra thought for a moment. The sooner they found Monterey and established the mission the better. He thought that very probably the ship would reach Monterey first.

"Very well," he agreed, "we will be waiting for you at Monterey. You can be the first travelers to hear Mass at our new mission of San Carlos," he agreed smiling.

It was settled. Padre Parron and Padre Gomez were left in charge of San Diego. Padre Crespi would accompany the land expedition.

The ocean voyage was unexpectedly difficult. The voyagers ran into unforeseen bad weather. Thus Padre Serra was aboard more than six weeks. He took this opportunity to write letters, among them a special one to Padre Palou. He told of all their adventures and begged for news. There were rumors that Pope Clement XIII had died and that the new Pope elected was a Franciscan. The Friars were eager to know whether this were true.

The group going by land found the trip much easier this time. It was spring. The hills were very green. Wild fruits and flowers covered the land. The party reached a high land which they had observed on their first trip. They broke for camp here.

While the leaders were discussing their position, some of the men set out on all sides to explore the lovely land. When shouts and a commotion were set up throughout the camp, Portola paid little attention.

"No doubt the men have been hunting and captured some strange animal," he thought. They had already seen elks, which they had taken for buffalo the last time they were here.

But when the commotion did not die down and shouts of "The bay, the bay!" reached his ears, he rushed out to meet them.

"What was that?" he called, curious now.

"The bay, my Commandant," came the reply. "Monterey is found."

"Impossible!" he shouted. "We were all over this land last winter."

"But here it is!" the soldiers told him. And they led him, still protesting, over another hill. There, before him, was the proof. The curved bay of glittering sapphire water stretched out along the dazzling white shore. It was a breathtaking sight.

"I can hardly believe it," Portola exclaimed. "How close we came before without seeing it. How blind we were!"

By June 3 the *San Antonio* had docked at the Bay of Monterey, guided by the fires burning as signals on the shore. It was the feast of Pentecost. An altar was set up under an oak overhanging the bay, where Mass had been said more than a hundred and fifty years ago, for Vizcaino's men. The mission bells were hung. A cross and the royal standard were erected and Padre Serra sang Mass. In a joyous ceremony Commandant Portola formally took possession of the land for Spain.

The soldiers fired a salute. From the bay the *San Antonio* answered. Commandant Portola had carried out his mission successfully. He had served the King well. Now he could return to Mexico triumphantly.

Padre Serra's work as President of the California missions had just begun. When news of the discovery was brought to Mexico and then to Spain, few people knew that this success was due to the unfailing faith and determination of the little lame Franciscan.

Now the founding of the missions must begin in earnest. The very first problem that presented itself was the new military commander, Don Pedro Fages. He was put in charge of Monterey when Commandant Portola sailed back to Mexico. Whenever he could, he managed to disagree with the Friars.

"Perhaps it would be best to avoid arguments by separation," Padre Serra told Juan Crespi. Together they searched for a place not too far away from the presidio, as the military settlement was called.

About three miles away, on the banks of a river that had been named the Carmel by the Friars accompanying Vizcaino, they found a better place for their mission.

Slowly it began to take shape. There were long low buildings of yellow mud brick. With his own hands Padre Serra aided in the building. In the central court he placed a large wooden cross. Here he spent many hours in prayer.

The climate at Carmel was warm and pleasant the year round. The surroundings were beautiful. They reminded Padre Serra of his home in Majorca. He decided that the mission of San Carlos would be headquarters for the President of the missions. San Carlos in Carmel Mission was opened in December of 1771.

Within a few days' journey of Carmel, Padre Serra founded a mission dedicated to San Antonio. The land was blessed with fertile soil. From its founding in July, 1771, this mission grew more rapidly than any other.

During the same year Padre Serra had the mission of San Gabriel founded, about nine miles from the place where the city of Los Angeles stands today. And between there and San Antonio he founded San Luis Obispo the following year.

El Camino Real was taking shape the way Padre Serra had planned. Now there were five settlements at which travelers might stop along the Royal Road. Some day, he hoped, there would be a continuous chain of missions up and down the coast within a day's journey of one another.

New missionaries were pouring in and the Indians were responding. Padre Junipero Serra could be proud of his work. But the hardships were far from over. In 1772 famine struck.

The Indians who had begun to build their huts near the missions had never farmed before. They lived by hunting wild game and eating roots and berries. Grain was planted and lessons in farming began. But by summer the food situation was desperate.

"What can we do, Padre?" asked one of the Friars, reporting to Padre Serra. "We have hardly enough flour to last a week. There is no meat. Perhaps we should send to Mexico for supplies."

Padre Serra shook his head sadly. "No, by the time the supplies reached us we would all be dead. We will have to begin rationing our food. A little corn, flour and milk each day will have to do until we can find other food. I am going to speak to Commandant Fages."

At the presidio Padre Serra told Fages of his fears. "We must have food to keep us until the autumn harvest. Perhaps a hunting party," he suggested.

"A hunting party!" exclaimed the Commandant. "What shall we hunt — rabbits?"

"Even rabbits would be a welcome sight," replied Padre Serra quietly.

Then Commandant Fages had an idea that would save them. He had heard the soldiers speak of a valley where a large number of bears had been seen. The Indians knew the place well, but they never hunted these animals. Their weapons were not deadly enough to kill such large beasts.

"It will be a different story with our muskets," decided Commandant Fages. He hurriedly organized the bear hunt. The Friars prayed for the successful and safe return of the hunters.

It was hard to await them patiently. Everyone avoided any mention of food.

Commandant Fages and his men remained in the Valley of the Bears for more than two months. They sent back a few loads of bear meat regularly. In the eyes of the Indians the Commandant had become a great hero. But he was not a hero to his men.

The soldiers considered him unreasonable and unnecessarily strict. Often they complained to the Friars of this. When Padre Serra tried to warn Fages to be more lenient, he only became very angry.

Word had reached Padre Serra that on at least two occasions soldiers had deserted and gone to live in the hills. They had returned only at the request and persuasion of the missionaries.

On the other hand, Padre Serra thought Fages was actually lax and disinterested when his men committed outrageous crimes against the Indians.

Once a group had cut off an Indian's head and placed it on a pole to warn other Indians of what would happen if they disobeyed the white men. This incident took place outside the Mission San Gabriel and was reported to Padre Serra. The Father President complained to Fages.

Fages only shrugged. "Well, the Indians should learn that they cannot disobey us. Perhaps it is a good thing." Padre Serra was shocked and saddened. How could the missionaries teach the religion of love when the Spaniards acted brutally?

In October of 1772 Padre Serra was in San Diego, having traveled on foot from Monterey. On the way he had founded San Luis Obispo. He was pleased with this progress, but as time went on Fages interfered more and more with the work of the missionaries. Padre Serra had reason to believe that the Viceroy did not understand the difficulties the missionaries were having with Fages. Certainly, if the Viceroy knew this, something would have been done by now. Fages insisted that he, and not the Friars, was in full charge of the missions. If this went on much longer, all the good work the missionaries had accomplished might be lost.

"Something must certainly be done," the missionaries at San Diego told the Father President. "Fages is even standing in the way of your founding new missions. Unless you receive the necessary soldiers, animals and supplies, nothing can be done."

Padre Serra was sitting at the writing desk in a sparsely furnished room. Now he stood, for there would be no place in the tiny cell for the other three missionaries to be seated. The tiny room contained only a desk and the wooden slab upon which the Friar slept. The little Franciscan was no longer in the prime of life. He was near his fifty-ninth birthday. His lame leg had never healed, and on his face tired lines could be seen. Yet he was still the determined missionary he had always been.

Just a few minutes before, he had just begun another letter to the Viceroy in Mexico City, but he put aside his quill as the missionaries entered the cell.

"You are right, Father. I am afraid that there is only one thing to do now. One of us must go to Antonio Bucareli. Perhaps if he learns of our difficulties at first hand, he will be better able to help us. It is too bad that our friend Galvez had to return to Spain," he sighed.

Padre Dumetz was concerned. "You are the one who must go, Padre. But such a long journey. You should take things easier now. You should rest more."

Padre Serra only smiled. "I think that such rest will not be mine in this life. After all we did not become missionaries because we wanted an easy life."

On October 20, 1772, Padre Serra took the boat to San Blas, Mexico. With him as companion he took an Indian convert whom he had baptized at Mission San Carlos. Juan Evangelista was a fine young man. He was most devout. Padre Serra thought that he was an excellent example of the work the missionaries were carrying on in Upper California.

Juan was happy to make the trip. He was very excited at the prospect of seeing Mexico City. He never tired of hearing Padre Serra tell stories of this wonderful place.

From San Blas, Padre Serra and Juan set out on foot. But on reaching Guadalajara, they both became terribly ill with a fever. Although the Friars there took good care of them, they became convinced that Padre Serra and his companion would not get well. Padre Serra must have thought so too, for he sent ahead a letter to the Viceroy, telling again of the serious dangers to the missions.

When all hope had been given up, the Friars prepared for the two to receive Holy Viaticum. Padre Serra did not pray for his own recovery. He thought only of poor Juan and his family at Carmel.

Then suddenly, almost miraculously, God answered Padre Serra's prayers. Both recovered and were able to continue on their way to Mexico City. Just before they arrived Padre Serra became ill a second time. Once again God spared him.

At Mexico City the new Viceroy, Antonio Bucareli, did not know what to make of the small Friar who had come such a great distance just to see him. Surely the Father President need not have come personally. Such a long journey for one his age, and lame besides, must have been torture. And when he learned of the Padre's illness and astonishing recovery, he could not help being impressed.

"Now Padre," he began, "I want you to think of me as your friend. Tell me, what can be so important that you had to come all the way from Monterey to see me?" He smiled kindly into the Friar's direct, truthful eyes.

Encouraged, Padre Serra told him all that had happened and how, with Fages in charge, the building of the missions was almost at a standstill. He also pleaded the cause of the unhappy soldiers. The Viceroy listened carefully. When Padre Serra had finished, Bucareli sat back silently for some time. At last he said:

"I am distressed by this unhappy state of affairs. If you would be good enough to put this report into writing, we will see what can be done. By the way, if it is decided to replace the Commandant, whom would you suggest?"

Padre Serra thought for a moment. "I would recommend a man who has proved himself both brave and very sympathetic to our problems. That man is Jose Francisco Ortega," he stated positively.

The Viceroy's eyes opened wide in surprise. He was amazed that the priest would suggest that Ortega should be raised to such an important position, but he said nothing.

Over the years the Father President had learned that patience was needed in all government matters. Now again he had to summon up as much as he could. The Viceroy kept him waiting several months. But the waiting was well worth it. He found that the Viceroy had really granted most of his requests. New orders were given for the establishment of missions at San Francisco and the long-promised San Buenaventura.

Commandant Fages was recalled and Captain Rivera was to take his place. Although this was not Padre Serra's choice, it meant at least some progress. The Father President went to thank Bucareli before he left. The Viceroy only waved this gratitude aside.

"If you really want to thank me, you will obey my orders. Your stubbornness is almost a legend. Now I have ordered a coach to carry you back to Guadalajara. You have been very ill and I have consulted your superiors about this. So you can see — there will be no arguments."

Padre Serra could do nothing but agree. He returned to Monterey. It was almost two years since he had left Mission San Carlos in Carmel. He was hopeful that now the mission work would run more smoothly.

Chapter Ten

The first martyr of the missions had given up his life.

X . . . . . The Missions' First Martyr

PADRE Serra was most anxious to reach San Carlos. For he knew that a very old friend would be there waiting for him. When they were face to face at last, he could hardly believe his eyes. The man was older and thinner, yes. But it was he!

"Francisco," he cried joyously. "Can it really be?" And the old Friar took off his glasses and wiped the tears from his eyes.

It had been so long since the two friends had been together that they hardly stopped talking for a moment. Dominican missionaries had now taken over the missions in Lower California. While Padre Serra had been in Mexico, Francisco Palou had been sent to San Carlos to act in the Father President's place.

"Here — you are tired," said Padre Palou at last. "We don't have to make up for all these years in an hour. There will be time for that. Now that I am here to stay for a while, you can talk my ears off."

They both laughed. Padre Serra was delighted to have his friend beside him again.

Along *El Camino Real* the missions grew and prospered. At San Diego Padre Luis Jayme was in charge. He was a very gentle young missionary and the Indians grew to love him. Padre Serra was very pleased with his work.

In the autumn of 1775 the harvest was very good. To add to Padre Jayme's joy, the number of baptisms had increased steadily. Earlier Padre Jayme had written to Padre Serra, requesting permission to have the mission moved to a hill about four miles from the presidio. Here there was more water and the farming was better.

The Indians loved Padre Jayme. They became accustomed to his familiar greeting: "*Amad a Dios, mis hijos* — Love God, my children."

At that time there were nine white men, including the two Friars, and two boys at the mission. One of the boys was Lieutenant Ortega's son, the other his nephew. There were also the Christian Indians who lived and worked diligently at the mission under the direction of the Friars. Two of them, Joachin and Francisco, were very quiet. They worked hard and said little. Then one day they disappeared.

"What could have happened?" worried Padre Fuster.

You could always trust Padre Jayme to look on the happy side. "Perhaps they have gone to bring some of their friends and relatives to be instructed," he suggested happily.

But Padre Fuster was still worried. Perhaps the work at the missions had been going along a little too smoothly. He wished he could talk all this over with Padre Serra.

For some reason Joachin and Francisco could not accept the missionaries' kindness. Perhaps they were incited by the devil himself. They were certain that the Spaniards had all come to make slaves of them. This they meant to stop. They went about telling other Indians that the Friars meant to force all of them to become Christians and would make slaves of them. Those who believed the story decided to destroy the missionaries.

And so, on the night of November 5, 1775, Joachin and Francisco returned. They brought with them a huge war party, in all nearly a thousand, including many Indian women. Daring and wild with excitement, they were bent on the destruction of the entire mission.

The shrewd Indians had seen their opportunity when some of the soldiers at the presidio set out with Lieutenant Ortega to help open another mission. With only four soldiers left at the mission itself, and with the presidio four miles distant, Mission San Diego was poorly guarded.

The mission slept peacefully beneath the clear, moonlit sky. Posting armed guards around the living quarters so that none of the Christian Indians could escape, the terrorists began their destructive work. Silently they stole into the church and tore down the statues and the altar. They carried away the vestments and seized the ornaments. Then, shrieking wildly, they threw firebrands at the thatched roofs of the buildings. Too late the sleepers awoke. Unfortunately the night guard at the presidio did not see the fires at the mission hill in time to send help. The blaze went unnoticed at first because of the strong light of the moon.

"May God have mercy on us. We are lost," cried Padre Fuster. He gathered the two boys to him.

Padre Jayme, on hearing the shouting and the crackling of the fire, stood up resolutely. "Perhaps the Indians will listen to me," he said bravely.

Swiftly the young missionary disappeared outside. The last thing the others heard from him was his gentle greeting to the savages: *"Amad a Dios, mis hijos."*

A furious battle raged for hours. One of the blacksmiths was killed almost at once. A young corporal held the Indians off by his deadly marksmanship, killing some and wounding others. When at last they had gone, it was nearly morning and the mission was almost entirely destroyed.

They looked for Padre Jayme and they found that the first martyr of the missions had given up his life. The Indians had tortured him before he died. He was buried in the chapel of the presidio, since the mission chapel was no longer standing.

Commandant Rivera received the news of Padre Jayme's martyrdom at Monterey and went at once to Mission San Carlos to bring the sad news to Padre Serra. The Father President wanted to go to San Diego as soon as possible after saying a requiem Mass for the honored martyr. But Rivera forestalled the Friar's departure.

"Your Reverence will understand that my men and I must go today, at once. We can wait for no one, and we can take no companions. As military commander I must bring protection for the presidio and begin an investigation without delay," he explained. "We shall probably ride all the way without dismounting."

When the Father President asked if he might hope for a military escort soon, Rivera replied no, because that would mean leaving too few soldiers at Monterey. Thus it was six months after he heard the news before Padre Serra arrived at the ruined mission.

Padre Serra worried a great deal about reports that reached him of the zeal with which the Commandant was going about punishing the Indians. He felt that what the Indians had done had been largely the result of their ignorance. He was afraid that the angry military leader would not take this into account.

Unfortunately, his fears were justified. Rivera reprimanded Lieutenant Ortega sharply for not acting quickly in punishing the Indians.

Rivera took his men and went out in search of the leaders of the attack. So strong was his feeling about punishing the Indians that he committed a terrible sin. One Indian returned to the church to seek refuge there. He was sorry, he told the Friars. He wanted forgiveness, which they gladly gave. He should have been safe then, for the law of the Church is that anyone who seeks refuge in a Catholic church may not be removed by force.

"Ridiculous!" announced Rivera. "Can anyone call a ruin a church? Besides, this building was originally a warehouse."

And he dragged the Indian away to prison. The priests were shocked. Such an action meant excommunication for Rivera. Even Lieutenant Ortega could not sympathize with the angry Commandant.

Padre Serra had tried to make Rivera see that he was wrong. "To ignore the law of sanctuary is a terrible thing. You must release this Indian at once," he directed.

But the military leader would not listen.

When the Father President arrived in San Diego early in July, he was faced with many problems. Foremost in his mind was the desire to rebuild the mission at San Diego. He found that there had been no further difficulties with the Indians and that Rivera was planning to send the chief culprits back to San Blas for punishment. Padre Serra felt that this would be a mistake. He thought that the Indians should be released in the custody of the missionaries. In this way the Friars could instruct the pagans and show them why they had been wrong. But because of Rivera's action nothing could be done about this now.

Padre Serra found that the missionaries were far from discouraged by the tragedy. "It is only that we are not able to carry on our work," they told him. For even though military reinforcements had arrived, nothing had been done about rebuilding the mission.

"Why rebuild the mission when these hostile Indians are only awaiting an opportunity to destroy it again?" Rivera had asked. "I cannot risk my men's lives on such a dangerous project." It looked as though Padre Serra was right back where he had been with Fages.

Then the *San Antonio* sailed into the harbor. Seeing the captain, whose name was Diego Choquet, gave Padre Serra an idea. He appealed to this goodnatured seaman. The priest told him all about his problems.

"Well, Diego, what do you say? Will you and your men help rebuild the mission of your own patron saint?" he begged.

Captain Choquet was flattered. Besides, he liked this gentle Friar with the determined eyes. "Certainly we will help," he promised gladly. "I daresay my men and I can do an excellent job and the fastest one you ever saw."

The work began and progressed rapidly. But Commander Rivera was not pleased. He resented what he considered to be Padre Serra's trick. One day he rode over to speak with Diego Choquet.

"I think you should be warned, Captain," he said angrily.

"Warned?" inquired Diego lazily.

"Yes, warned," replied Rivera firmly. "We have heard that the Indians plan to attack again. You are in great danger."

Captain Choquet looked him in the eye. "Why, Commandant!" he said boldly, trying to act surprised. "If you are so worried about our safety, why don't you provide us with more guards instead of showing this womanish fear?"

Angry and embarrassed, Rivera rode away. But Rivera had his way. Captain Choquet and his men were forced to stop. Sadly they sailed back to San Blas without finishing their work.

But not long afterward the Viceroy sent word that he was in favor of Padre Serra's position. Now Rivera had to listen. With the help of the Christian Indians, the Friars rebuilt the mission. The Viceroy also ordered that, as soon as arrangements could be made, Rivera was to return to Lower California. Governor Felipe de Neve himself was ordered to go to Monterey to see personally to the progress of the missions. Now *El Camino Real* grew rapidly. It was going to be the Golden Highway the Father President had envisioned.

For some time Padre Serra had wanted to found missions north of Monterey. "How long our Father St. Francis has had to wait for his mission," he had said many times.

Then Captain Anza arrived with orders to select a place for a mission and presidio near the excellent harbor of San Francisco. Padre Serra was so busy at San Diego that Padre Palou was sent to found Mission San Francisco de Asis. A rough chapel was set up and the bell hung. Today the bell is still rung in the mission, which stands in the heart of the beautiful city of San Francisco that grew up around it. Padre Palou erected the cross and blessed the site on October 9, 1776.

Additional guards were provided for all the missions. The mission of San Juan Capistrano was refounded. It had first been established a few days before the attack on San Diego. When news of the attack reached San Juan Capistrano, the soldiers left at once to help their countrymen in San Diego and the Friars accompanied them. The Capistrano mission bell had been buried. Now the Father President was very pleased with the progress that was being made with the refounding of this mission.

North of Monterey, building began on the mission of Santa Clara. It was established on January 12, 1777.

The missions were progressing very well, but now a new problem faced Padre Serra. The Spanish authorities wished to change the system of government within the missions. Some of them felt that by giving the Indians more freedom and allowing them to elect their own leaders they would not be so dependent on the missionaries and would be better off. Padre Serra knew that the Indians were not as yet ready for this. If this new policy were followed, he felt that it would mean the destruction of all that the Friars had achieved.

Many of the other Friars felt the same way. They were discouraged and did not want to continue their labors under such a system. Bad news seemed to follow Padre Serra as he toured the missions.

One day a Friar found Padre Serra very much upset over a letter he had received. "What can be the matter?" he inquired.

"The new system of government is causing even more trouble than I expected," he replied. "Some of the Friars are becoming discouraged because of it. Already we are very shorthanded, and now both Padre Lasuen and Padre Figuer have asked to be transferred."

The Father President wrote immediately to these two fine missionaries, begging them to stay. He must have been very convincing because it was Padre Lasuen himself who later became Father President of the missions.

As for the new system of government, it did not work out as the Spaniards expected. And soon Padre Serra was gratified to find that Governor de Neve no longer was trying to enforce it.

In 1782 Padre Serra was saddened by the loss of his friend Padre Juan Crespi. His former student and beloved companion died on New Year's Day. They had been together for many years. Long ago Padre Serra had learned that in time of sorrow work was a great comfort to him. On Easter Sunday of that year he founded San Buenaventura. It was to be the last of the golden chain of missions that stretchd along *El Camino Real* that he would himself establish.

It was San Buenaventura for which Inspector General Galvez had been packing when he raced with Padre Serra so long ago.

"It seems strange," Padre Serra thought, "that this was one of the first missions we planned and here it is the ninth to be established." He found special happiness in the founding of this beloved mission.

He was pleased, too, that he had been able to confirm many of the Indians. The Pope had given him a special faculty or permission to do so. It was practically impossible for a Bishop to visit Upper California, because there was already too much work for the few Bishops in Mexico. Besides, the journey could not have been undertaken often enough by the Mexican Bishops.

As the missions grew and prospered, Padre Serra grew old. He felt that soon God would call him. In the summer of 1783 he decided to make the round of his nine missions. Perhaps this would be his last opportunity to administer the sacrament of Confirmation to those of his "children" who had not yet received the sacrament.

Although he had been ill and such a journey would mean many hardships, he decided to leave by boat for San Diego. Before he left, he wrote to Padre Palou.

"I am getting old, Francisco," he wrote. "Perhaps this is my last letter to you. The next news you receive may be the news of my death. But I am pleased with the way the missions are growing." Then he proceeded to leave a list of instructions for the next Father President.

Everywhere he went the Friars were glad to see him, but they were saddened by his weary appearance. During the past few years Padre Serra had developed a bad case of asthma. He was really very ill and it was clear to everyone that he would not live much longer.

From San Diego he went to San Juan Capistrano and San Gabriel, and then on to San Buenaventura. He was pleased with the number of Christian Indians he found at this new mission. He traveled on to San Luis Obispo, San Antonio and home to San Carlos. Here he stayed during Lent and also celebrated Easter before continuing his rounds. At Santa Clara he blessed the new church.

At last he arrived at San Francisco. How glad Padre Palou was to see him! He had been so worried by the last letter he had received. But Padre Serra appeared very strong and well. Unfortunately they did not have too much time together, for a priest whom they both admired was ill at Santa Clara and later died there. Padre Palou left for that mission at once and Padre Serra followed later.

By the time his special faculty to administer Confirmation ran out in July of 1784, Padre Serra had confirmed in all 5,308 persons.

Back at San Carlos again, Padre Serra seemed to have had a strange premonition. Perhaps he knew somehow that God would call him soon. He wrote farewell messages to all the missions and asked the nearest missionaries to come to him. To Father Palou he sent an urgent message. His old friend hurried to his side.

Padre Palou was saddened by the Father President's weakened condition. Nevertheless, he managed to be cheerful.

"Well now that I am here, I shall see to it that you rest more often," he told the old Padre firmly. "I don't expect to have any arguments either, because I am not afraid to point out that I am bigger than you are."

Padre Serra laughed shakily and agreed to rest a little. He knew that there would not be much more time left for him to be with his friend. He wasn't sad. It was enough happiness to have Padre Palou near him, even for a little while.

Chapter Eleven

Kneeling in the little adobe church, Padre Serra received Our Lord for the last time.

XI . . . . . The Golden Highway

PADRE Serra stretched himself after his night's rest. It was nearly daybreak and the soft light of dawn found its way through the little window into the tiny bare room. He drew his one rough blanket over his narrow wooden bed and set out for the church to say the first Mass of the day.

He walked very slowly, for his leg was troubling him. Sometimes it was difficult for him to breathe. He paused in prayer before the large wooden cross in the courtyard. There was a great deal of pain in his chest this morning, but he paid little attention to it.

When the mission bells began to sound their morning call, he looked up and smiled to see the birds fly hurriedly out of the belfry. They had been rudely frightened from their home.

Two Indian altar boys met him at the church. "Good morning, Padre," they greeted him. One of them stared solemnly with his dark eyes upon the old missionary's face.

"Are you feeling better this morning, dear Padre?" he inquired hopefully.

"Why, I am not ill! Don't look so worried or you will convince me that I am, little one," said Padre Serra cheerfully.

The words were reassuring, but nevertheless the little Indian boy continued to watch the old Padre with sad eyes all during Mass. When his beloved friend had a fit of coughing, the child's heart was filled with terror.

Later Padre Palou found the Indian child sitting on the church steps crying. "What is it, my son?" he asked kindly.

"Oh, Padre Francisco, the old Padre is so sick," the boy told him tearfully. "Soon he will go away to his home in heaven."

Padre Palou knew this was true. He could see that his friend was growing weaker every day. Now he went looking for him and found the Father President, looking pale, but happily helping the small children with their catechism lesson.

"Padre Junipero, you absolutely must rest. Your altar boys tell me that you were ill this morning."

"Francisco, you should know by now that I cannot sit idly while there is still work to be done," he told Padre Palou gently, going right ahead with the lesson.

There was nothing for Padre Palou to do with his determined friend. The mission was really growing rapidly. Many conversions had been made. Once an Indian was baptized he was expected to live at the mission. Everyone had work to do. The men were farmers and the women busied themselves making clothes. It had been a struggle, but the Friars had seen to it that the men were properly clothed.

In the past Padre Serra had liked to help with the sewing. He would sit on the floor among the women and girls and cut the cloth for the blouses and skirts. Fondly they teased him.

Classes went on all day. And the children were always delighted to have the old Padre teach them. They leaned against him and clasped his hands, gazing into his loving face while he told stories of Jesus.

But now Padre Serra could spend less time with them. His condition grew steadily worse. Even so he still led the devotions for the neophytes himself. It was at these times that Padre Palou thought the old Padre seemed much improved. But a soldier who had been with Padre Serra a long time did not share this opinion.

"The Father President always seems well when he is praying and singing, Your Reverence," he warned. "But do not be deceived. He is very ill."

The royal physician, who had come to the mission to see the Father President, had ordered hot poultices to be applied to the Padre's chest.

These were painful and must have caused him much discomfort. But Padre Serra gave no sign of this. He continued to act as though he were not sick at all, doing what he could to share the duties of the Friars at the mission.

On August 25 he sent for Padre Palou. The priest hurried to his friend's side. "What is it, Your Reverence? You seem upset. Do you feel worse?"

"I am as well as usual, Francisco," answered the old Padre gently. "But I am worried. I wrote to San Antonio and San Luis Obispo, asking the Friars there to come to receive supplies for the missions and to bid me farewell. Still they are not here. Do you think that the letters could have been delayed?"

Padre Palou made inquiries at once. He found that the letters had been accidentally mislaid and not yet delivered. He dispatched them immediately, adding a plea of his own for haste.

Now Padre Palou was certain that his friend expected to die very soon. Sadly he gave up any hopes he had for the Father President's recovery.

Although the messages were rushed to the neighboring missionaries, the Friars were not able to arrive at San Carlos in time. Two days later Padre Serra asked to receive Holy Viaticum.

Padre Palou forced back the tears that came to his eyes. Keeping his voice as steady as possible, he said, "Of course, Your Reverence. I will have your cell prepared so that Our Lord can come to you there."

But Padre Serra surprised him by refusing. "No, Francisco," he said softly. "I can still walk to the church. There is no need for Our Lord to come to me. I will go to Him."

Padre Palou was astonished. He had never heard of such a thing. Holy Viaticum was always brought *to* the sick. But then he never ceased to be amazed by Padre Serra's humility and courage.

The Commandant and some of the soldiers from the presidio along with all the Christian Indians of the mission witnessed a very beautiful and unusual ceremony that afternoon. Kneeling in the little wooden church before the altar of Our Lady, Padre Serra received Our Lord for the last time. The church glowed with the light of the candles held by the soldiers and the Indians. Padre Serra himself sang the *Tantum ergo.* All were inspired by his strength and piety.

That night was a difficult one for Padre Serra and a sad one for his friends. He did not lie down upon his customary bed of rough boards. Most of the time he spent on his knees, with his chest pressed against the boards of the bed to get a little relief. Sometimes he sat on the floor, leaning against the lap of his Indian neophytes, who wanted to stay close to their "father." The Indians watched over him with great tenderness.

During the night he received the holy sacrament of Extreme Unction. For this ceremony he sat on a little stool made of rushes. The next afternoon he finally consented to lie down on his bed. Padre Palou was glad that his friend wanted to rest at last. He tiptoed from the room.

But when he returned, later in the afternoon, he found that Padre Serra was indeed sleeping. It was the long, eternal sleep. God had called His servant.

Mournfully the mission bells began to toll their sad tidings. All the mission work ceased. Friars, Indians, soldiers and sailors gathered sadly to say their last farewells to the little Friar who had given his life for them. He was seventy years old. It had been a long and fruitful life.

That Sunday, after a long procession, his body was laid beside that of Padre Juan Crespi in the church of San Carlos. He was buried in the sanctuary, on the Gospel side. Later the church was rebuilt of stone, and many years after that, when it fell into ruins, it was again restored. But Padre Serra's body remained buried there and his tomb may be seen at San Carlos even today.

After the burial service Padre Palou told everyone of Padre Serra's last promise.

"Our Father President said that if God chose to bring him to heaven, he would continue to pray for the success of the missions and the conversion of the Indians."

The loss of Padre Serra weighed heavily upon the missions. They were like sheep who had lost their shepherd. Almost immediately after Padre Serra died, people began begging Padre Palou to give them some little remembrance, something that had belonged to their beloved father. Padre Palou did what he could, giving them two handkerchiefs and the Padre's inner tunic.

Stories of almost miraculous incidents connected with these objects reached Padre Palou. The royal physician, who had one of the handkerchiefs, reported:

"One of my men was suffering from violent headaches that made him quite ill and unable to sleep. Nothing I could do would help. Then I fastened our beloved Padre Serra's handkerchief about his head, when he woke next morning the pain was gone."

Another such incident Padre Palou witnessed himself. Padre Paterno, who had been summoned by the Father President before his death, arrived at the mission too late even for the funeral. He was an older man, and the heat of August in addition to the hasty journey had weakened him. He became seriously ill, and Padre Palou was thinking of administering the Last Rites of the Church. Then he had an idea.

"Would you like me to give you Padre Serra's hairshirt to wear?" he asked. Padre Paterno accepted gratefully. Not long afterward he was well again.

Whether or not these were miraculous cures and revealed Padre Serra as one of God's saints, Padre Palou did not know. He did know that his friend had accomplished a great deal during his life and had served God well. He began to write down everything he knew about

Padre Serra and the founding of the missions. Padre Palou's life of the great missionary is still one of the most important books we have about Junipero Serra.

Little Miguel Jose Serra had grown into a man of great strength and endurance. Lame and no longer young, he had started out on a long road in a strange and untamed land. He had changed this rough road into a Royal Road — a truly Golden Highway dedicated to the King of kings, Our Lord. Now Padre Serra's missions stretched like a chain of faith up and down the coast of California.

Along the way men had been discouraged. Some had turned back and given up. But Padre Serra remained, determined to bring the souls of the Indians to God. He had led his missionaries onward, inspiring them by his faith and enthusiasm.

Today the missions still stand, although many have had to be restored and rebuilt. Visitors to California can follow *El Camino Real,* and see the missions that stand forever as a tribute to the zeal of this brave little Friar.

For Padre Junipero Serra had a valuable secret. He knew that with God's help even a little lame Friar could be as big as anyone, inside.

SAN DIEGO
UNITED
VELICATA
LOWER CALIFORNIA
Gulf of California
GUADALUPE
LA PURISIMA
LORETO
SAN FRANCISCO XAVIER
La Paz Bay
LA PAZ
Cape San Lucas
M
SAN BL
TEPIC
Pacific Ocean
Lower (BAJA) California and Mexico